Inspirationally Redeemed

I0149599

Dwayne J. Torres

Andrea Johnson Books Publishing

Inspirationally Redeemed

Cover art designed by Andrea Johnson Books Publishing.

First published by Andrea Johnson Books Publishing. 1/8/2019

6565 N. MacArthur Blvd, Suite 225 Dallas, TX. 75039
www.Ajbpublishing.com

All poems written produced and composed by Dwayne J. Torres, with the exception of: 'Inspirationally Redeemed' written by Dwayne J. Torres & Andrea Johnson Torres. 'King's Ransom' written by Dwayne J. Torres & Dwayne Torres II. 'Kanye's Prayer' written by Dwayne Torres II.

ISBN: 978-0-578-43850-4

Introduction

This is a relational, emotional, and spiritual book which speaks to the spirit and the broken. Each poem was spiritually written with the inspiration of Love and the Holy Spirit.

It talks to your inner man/woman. It speaks to your soul, and ignites a passion in you which you've never known before.

By the time you finish reading, you'll want a relationship with our Lord and Savior Jesus Christ. You'll thirst for that peace which your spirit yearns daily.

- Minister Dwayne J. Torres

Acknowledgements

First and Foremost, I Want to thank God, the Father, for the unlimited amount of blessings that you've bestowed upon me. For Blessing me with the gift of life and of words. Using me to encourage my fellow brothers and sisters with an attitude of love and thanksgiving. Thank you, Father God, for choosing me to be a part of this life for such a time as this.

I also want to thank My Beautiful Queen Andrea, for her Love, Patience, and Support. We've traveled a mighty long way and the road has never gotten easy. Which means that we are on the right path, because we are creating our own. You're my number one cheerleader and full Royalty Support System. You are truly My Greatest Blessing, I Love You Baby.

To my mother Mama Ghee, you were my first Teacher, Preacher, Doctor, Lawyer, but most of all, you are My Mother. You have been such a great inspiration in my life, you always believed in me, and told me two things. Never Kiss anybody's nether regions, and don't take this life for granted. That no matter how tough my life gets, if I could talk about it the next day, then I am blessed.   Thank You Mama Ghee for your Love, I Love You.

To my oldest son Dwayne II, who I call Mr. Wisdom. Since you were born it was us against the world. I've watched you grow up to be a fine Young King with a wisdom beyond your age bracket. You have a lot to offer, so Let God Use you, to be the bright star that's needed in this dark world. Daddy loves you.

To my oldest daughter Alidra, daddy loves you, continue to be the blessing you are to your peers, and family alike. You are more than a conqueror, and My Young Queen.

To my middle child Imani, you are the one with the Heart of Gold. You have such a testimony untold, I cannot wait till your future unfolds. Because you're the one standing Bold. God bless you My Young Queen, for his love will always have a hold. Daddy Loves You.

To my youngest and The Most Daring Son, Michael, what can I say other than you are a true Champion. You are who God says that you are, not what man tries to dictate for you to be. Continue to grow up to be the Warrior that your Nana, proclaimed for you to be. Daddy loves you Young King.

To my baby girl Talitha, the Angel of the Family. Your faith is immeasurable, and your wisdom is amazing. There were times when you, yes you, helped me realize how blessed that I really am. Even when life takes a toll, your smile and faith, helps keep me going. Thank you, Young Queen, for being daddy's little Angel. I Love you Baby Girl.

To all of my Family, Sister, Brother, Cousins, Nephews, Aunties, Uncles, Grandparents, Great Grandparents, Friends. Thank you for making my life a joy. Knowing that I've come from a family of greats, puts an extra stamp of blessings. I love you all Forever – Uncle Joe, Joe-Cool.

To all of my extended families from, Ronald Edmonds JHS, Robeson High School, BMCC, New Canaan Baptist Church, Pentecostal House of Prayer, Manhattan Bible Institute, The Potter's House, PHSOM, Met-Ed, Colgate-Palmolive, and Liberty Mutual. For those who I've met on Instagram, Facebook, and Twitter, I want to thank you all for being a part of my Journey called life. God Bless you all, I Love you guys, and as always, Be Blessed and be a Blessing.

My Dedication to all whom these words may touch...

This Book is dedicated to the depressed, oppressed, the sick, and for those who feel hopeless. I pray that this book shows you of what and who God wants you to be. God has blessed me with the gift of poetry, and being that God has given me this gift, I am going to share it with the world. To remind you that there is no sin that God cannot cover, no weapon formed against you, and your sins are already forgiven.

Stop judging yourself, and stop living in the past. You don't live there anymore, neither does your future. According to God's Word, your Future is Greater than your past. Haggai 2:9. Remember, you are his greatest creation, you were meant to build a nation.

A nation filled with a legacy that is true, everyday speak something new. Speak life into your future, and watch how you'll succeed. There's no need to speak of haters, because even your flesh can be your greatest debater.

I pray that this book speaks to you and your soul. This book is dedicated to you, my brothers and sisters. May God continue to bless you and may Heaven smile upon you.

Table of Contents

Who Am I? 174

I'm a soul survivor*Am I still relevant?*Tired King, messenger developer*The identity crisis*Know who you are*Validation* Look at me I'm soaring*My name is*My name is 2*My name is 3*When I look at you, I see purpose*What next, where did I go wrong?* You are your greatest enemy*A kingdom man

Believer 192

Do you believe what you perceived? *The esteem of others* Blessed*Prayer*The true warrior*The virtuous woman*The journey*Whose life is it anyway? * The power of unity

From Soul to Soul

Dwayne J. Torres

Inspirationally Redeemed

Torn between two worlds, whether I'm going north or south, can you hear me lord, the praises that's coming out of my mouth? I speak the language, but I feel a shift. One is pulling me down, while the other uplifts. My goal is to reach up, but my flesh pulls me down. I have no feelings to my feet, am I walking on solid ground?

Tortured and consumed, left out and presumed dead. I claw my way through a depiction of what is real, versus what is said. Perhaps I was never created to aspire, my dreams touching a glass window held back within muck and fire. I'm convinced there's no use for me in a world submerged in visual stimulation. I have placed all my worth in a decreasing value they call a nation.

But his promise.

It is within a cold and dark world, that I find my true purpose. It is not to live for those that seek my service. I remember the promise of God's word, that he will keep me in all my ways. Lest I dash my foot against those that come to steal and take.

I am here not because of the derelict that you have planned for me. I don't have to live by the world's conformity.

You see I have been changed in ways that will keep me on the path, regardless of how impossible things may seem.

I am no longer what you have dictated I should be. I am inspirationally redeemed.

You Were Made To Prevail

Stagnate, is how you feel, facing against a nation. At times you feel it's best to stay in procrastination.

But that's not the Liberty in which you stand. You were created to be That Great Woman or That Great Man.

How can you defeat a demon so great? When he turns your faith into Fate?

Don't believe in the lie, believe in the Faith. Because it's not of yourselves for you to create.

It's not supposed to be easy, it's supposed to be possible. But you allow the fear to capture you at the beginning of probable.

But here is the truth, you need to know now. You were created for a purpose, not a someway, somehow.

You say that your sin is the cause of your stagnation. But it's really your fears that's creating the hallucination.

Jesus died so you can escape from the gates of hell. You were meant to be Champion, you were made to prevail.

It started out as an idea then it became a dream. You've placed a goal, and everything is upstream.

But doubt kicked in, because you exceeded other's expectations. They wanted you to live at their corner store, when you were meant to lead a Nation. Not saying that you're better, but they have their own race. You can't get distracted, by thriving at their pace. The dreamers can walk, but you were meant to fly. They're supposed to look at you, Soaring across the Skies. You are to fly to be their inspiration. Then reach out your hand and send them some Motivation. God's Grace was your escape from hell.

You were meant to be a Leader, you were made to prevail. Ok call it the air, heads or tails. Round 1, ring the Bell. All aboard, next stop is Your destiny. Last stop will be your sea of tranquility. Which means you've done your due, as well as had fun.

Praying to God that you'll hear the words "Well Done." Maximize your Moments, Live to be all you can be. Look at yourselves through God's Eyes, then truly live free. God never makes a promise that he doesn't keep. You live here on this Earth and not Beneath. Your Life has purpose, a legacy to Leave, a Generational Story to Tell. Your wings will soar, you will explore, you were Made to Prevail.

Don't Miss It Because You're Gifted

God: The Grass always seems greener, when they're not yours. You took an opportunity, but there was nothing but closed doors. You were made to believe, but instead you were deceived.

Don't be ashamed, by falling short. You've made a plan, but you had to abort. I know all about your mistakes. Not seeking wisdom, by trusting a snake.

There're too many things that you need to explore, put away your doubts, use faith forevermore.

You got the knowledge, you got the plan, make no excuses, just try to understand.

That where you're going is greater than now. I know what you can handle, so I won't allow.

Failure on a task that was promised. Live Obediently and honest.

I know your sins may hold you back. But Jesus died for you, so relinquish the attack.

The attack on your living and self-esteem. You are the goal, you are the dream.

I put together The Earth, The Sun, and The Moon. Even I rested on the 7th day too.

The world hears my message, but some got it twisted. Don't miss this Blessing, you are Gifted.

The world tells you that you need to do you. Which is ok, but why practice voodoo? They do it, because there's no trust in me. But I'm the one who delivers from all insecurities.

I've planted a road in you to create. Don't allow your idiosyncrasies to put you up for a debate.

Because you'll doubt, and you will hesitate. But you're the one I've chosen, the Best Candidate.

I've given you powers to make the devil quiver. Because when it comes to My Promises, I always Deliver.

Some may look at you as an over achiever. But I want them to see me in you and become a Believer.

I want them to know that they're a blessing as well. Together My Son Jesus and I will Protect them from Hell.

Again, I've chosen you because I did not want you to miss it. You've overcome every obstacle, because You're Gifted.

Healed

I was hurt in my past, a pain that I thought would forever last.

I dreamed that one day I would be complete. No longer living with defeat.

Now my story is becoming clearer, I'm not where I was last year.

I no longer hold on to the pain, I've let go my crazy and insane.

Because I've crippled myself for far too long, while singing the same old song.

Oh lord, oh lord, when am I going to be free? Is there a cure to my doubting, decaying, or oppressive disease?

All I had to do was look up and see. That Jesus has died for you and me.

My cure was in the form of my belief. There's purpose for all of my grief.

God raised the standard, when the flood was revealed. He Covered me under the blood, so now I am healed.

Dwayne J. Torres

I'm Your Thankful Servant

When you speak to the Mountain it'll be Moved. When you speak to Music, it enhances its Groove. When you speak to The Winds, it becomes Calm. When you say that I'm here, you say it with Opened Arms. You speak to Birds, they begin to fly. You speak to The Blind, and they Opened Their Eyes. You speak Life, and I began to Live it. When you spoke to My Soul, you gave me The Holy Spirit. Forgive me for the times I've lived in doubt. Forgive my tantrums, whenever I scream or Shout. I didn't understand my destination, or my story. I didn't even want to share my testimony. I couldn't accept your ways or your plans. I had to make decisions to show that I'm a Man. When I cry, they say that I'm weak. But you say that I am Strong, my Faith is starting to Speak.

My Faith has spoken because I started to Trust. Praising your name for me is a must. You've removed my fears, replaced it with Peace. Doubt has flown away, insecurities deceased. You brought me out from comfort to the unfamiliar. I give My Life to you lord, yes, I Surrender. Thank you for blessing me, especially when I don't deserve it. You've given me power over demons and serpents. Thank you, Father God, for your mercy and grace. I'll serve You Father God, while seeking your face. It's not about Me, it's about My Service. Forever Father God, I will humbly be, Your Thankful Servant.

Inspired by The Apostle Paul and The Book of Ephesians

God & Me

Dwayne J. Torres

Be Still and Know Me

I knew your name before your birth, I am the one who knows your very worth.

I took in your pain as well as your strife. I am the maker of your soul, I've given you life.

I am your Mother and your Father, as well as your Sister and Brother. I am the one who carries you through storms and mind clutter.

I'm your food when you fast, I am the sweat on your brow. I am your generations to come, I am the smile to your frown.

Although you don't feel me, I'm always there. I'm the one who listens to your tears, when no one else cares.

I could be your friend if you allow. I'm the one who fills you up, I'm the quiet to your loud.

I created each season, so you can appreciate each storm. Because it's really an elevation for you, to live above the norm.

Your flesh and devil cannot stop my purpose for your living. Which is why your soul stays in Thanksgiving.

Sometimes you can't hear me, because you allow your heart to be deceived. You listen to the worldly possessions thinking that you'll never achieve.

But get to know me because I am your source. I'll make sure that you'll stay on course.

It may not look like much because there are trees and rocks along the way. But you're the bulldozer to create the path to be a blessing to your staff you pay.

Your life was meant to be a blessing to others, not self-indulgent. I want you to live free, not Spiritually Ignorant.

If you trust me, your life becomes your dream come true. Behind every grey cloud is the sky color blue.

Remember that the very blessing you seek are the ones you don't see. Because if you saw what was in store, you would never believe.

This is why I don't require you, I just ask if you will. Trust in me and learn to be still.

For you'll never know what it can be. You know that I am he, I just want you to know me.

Why Are You Calling My Name?

Don't look at me Father, I am truly not worthy. I'm the one that's never satisfied and always worry.

Why are you calling me? I told you I don't deserve it. I take what I want because I believe that I'm worth it.

No Father, can't you see that I am a mess? Look how I treat people especially those who want to test.

I fornicate whenever I get the chance. I'm not even good enough to keep a Silent Romance.

Yes, I believe in you and all that you've done. But choosing me Father, huh I'm not the one.

I have too many flaws, and I haven't been to Church in Years. I am the one responsible for My Mother's Tears.

Because I stayed away, Gospel is something that I didn't want to hear. Because the Pastors in Church only preach about Money and Fear.

They say that I should fear you for what you can do. Then turn around and say that you're saying, "Hey My Child I Love You"

I don't want to be a part of something so phony and un-pure. Why are there so many diseases with no cure?

When it comes to money, I want it all. I even laugh at a Senior Citizen when they fall.

Inspirationally Redeemed

I want my cake and eat it too. I even compared people to the animals in the Zoo.

I am the Cream of the Crop when it comes to Social Media. I have more followers than the President and Socialite Divas.

But why are you still calling me, aren't I supposed to find you? Look at all the mess that I create and do.

I'm no better than a fool or drunken man. Sometimes I hate people worse than the Ku Klux Klan.

I've even murdered and then I ran away. My time is too precious, I cannot fit you into my day.

What do you want from me Father? I am no good to you or your people. When it comes to sin, I believe I'm Sodom and Gomorrah's Equal.

But look at my story, as to how many times I make mistakes. But you know me better than I, one touch is all it takes.

I'm sorry father, but you have to understand. I am a sinner whose life comes as it may without a goal or plan.

But Father God I know that you can help me, but I don't want it this way. I have yet to get myself straight, which I'll be someday.

But now is not the time, for I have so much work that needs to be done. But you said in your word that you gave us Your only begotten Son. Truth is Father, I feel so ashamed. Because I was looking for love from people, who didn't even know my name.

Father please forgive me, I hear you, and I want to come home. I'll call back my mother, and apologize, for telling her to leave me alone. This time Father God, I want to get it right. So, this time I'm reaching out to you, this day and night.

I know that you are listening to the words I say. So, Father God, I Give Myself Away.

After tonight, I am no longer the Same. Thank you Father God for Remembering and Calling My Name.

Much is Given, Much is Required

You were born with a purpose, and it's not to live in fear. You were born into greatness not to imitate the unsettled and unclear.

You see success as a monetary and materialistic wealth. But procrastinate at the notion while placing your talents on a shelf.

You look at other people's blessings and wondering where's yours? Not realizing that you are standing in front of its doors.

The Hall of Blessings that I have for you may not seem appealing. It looks as if you have to work harder by hustling and pipe dreaming.

But It's only harder because you're comparing and climbing the wrong ladder. Because if you just see what I'm doing in the Spirit, you'll see that it's your life that matters.

I've given authority and I've also given you a choice. I want you to listen in spirit, but you're listening to the wrong voice.

The voice of doubt and misunderstanding with a touch of grief. Wondering if you missed your mark by playing with life's trick or treat.

The trick of the enemy makes you believe in a treat. But it's all a set up for a mind's defeat.

Take off the robe of worry, and the cutting corner of desires. In order to fulfill your destiny, Much is Given, Much is Required.

Requirement number one is the freeing of the mind. Realizing that you're uniquely designed.

Requirement number two, forget about your past. For only what you do for Christ will truly last.

Requirement number three, step aside and allow God. Trust that he is there even when life gets hard.

Just listen to me, and I already have a plan. For you to have an abundant life, your wings will expand.

Soaring across the skies where the Eagles fly. Still up high even when you're on a dive.

Because you've paid the cost, you've exceeded friendly fire. Now wear your crown, of Much Given, Much Required.

Inspirationally Redeemed

Into Your Hands Lord, I Command My Spirit

Flesh: I was found not guilty, but I'm still in Prison. I guess I have to be more careful of My Decisions.

Look, you told me to trust you. But it wasn't in line of what I wanted to do.

Ok true, it's not about me. But how can one succeed?

When excuses keep coming out of My Mouth. You told me to go North, I went South.

It's not that I didn't listen. But the world made me feel as if there was something missing.

The good life, the cars, the women, the money. But Living from Check to Check truly isn't Funny.

Your word says that you want me to prosper. But you act as if you don't want to be bothered.

I'm Living in Hell, a World of No Good. Living in poverty and in Ghetto Neighborhoods.

I know that I could get out. But that's not what Our Schools Teaches Us About.

I'm Living a Lie, I should just roll up and die.

When I Pray, you don't hear it. Into Your Hands Lord, I Command My Spirit.

God: You're not in Prison, but your mind lives there. How can you say that you're not prospering, when I supply Your Air?

You take for granted about the life you have. You live as if your flag is up Half-Staff.

You never want for nothing because I supply Your Needs. Following a Chicken when you're an Eagle, you can't succeed.

You settled for the Ground when you were made to Soar. I've given you Talents and Gifts which you have Ignored.

If you seek me first, Everything Will Be Added unto you. Transforming Your Mind is something you should do.

Your leaders removed me from schools, and I was never brought back. Criticized a child For Praying Over His Lunch Sack?

But I won't take your Life, because you're there for a purpose. To be a blessing to all, with your Smile and Service.

Once you fulfill your obligations, it'll be My Pleasure. To accept you back home to your Mansions and Treasure.

Your Prayers? Yes, I do hear It. Into My Hands Lives Grace and Your Spirit.

Inspirationally Redeemed

Because I'm A Praying Man

I Don't Claim to Be Perfect, But I Do Stand Tall. I Know Where My Help Cometh, Even When I Fall. I'm Not Always Righteous, But I Strive to Be. Even When I Sin, Jesus Sets Me Free. Whenever I Get Blessed, There's A Cost. I Find My Way Back to God, Even When I'm Lost. Glory to God, For Never Abandoning Me.

Removing Spiritual Blinders, So I Can See. That the Walk in This Life, Is About Him Alone. With Every Prayer Reaching, To His Throne. I Get My Powers, From A Position on Ground Zero. I Get Up with An Anointing, I'm My Family's Superhero. I Don't Expect Everyone to Fully Understand. I am Favored, Because I'm A Praying Man.

Living This Life Is Tough, Because I'm Always Under Attack. Living the Blessed Life, Because the Blood of Jesus Has My Back. The Journey Is Longer, Distractions on Every Side. Devil Speaks So Loudly, I've Listened to Pride. But What God Has Promised, I Will Reach There. No Matter How Much Satan Suffocates, I'll Breathe My Destiny's Air.

God is in Control, Which Means There's Victory. Fasting and Supplication, Truly Completes Me. My Reward is Entering into His Presence. My Spirit Prays, With Great Substance. Because Sometimes, I Don't Know What to Pray For. But My Soul Prayers, Always Reaches God's Door. Because it Understands Exactly What I Need. Humbly, Boldly, Down on Bended Knees. My Good Always Out Weighs My Bad.

His Ultimate Love Is Something We've Always Had. I Pray and Hope That You and Yours Will Forever Stand. And That The Anointing Destroys Your Yokes, For I Am A Praying Man.

I'm A Praying Man 2

You see My Tears as Weakness, I see it as Strength. There's a swelling to the pain, My Faith Reaching Great Lengths. You criticize My God, you say he's not real. Because you see me struggling, you claim the devil and I made a deal. Only a fool would sell his soul. Just for a temporary mind control. That's not how I flow, because I rather be living. Victoriously, Confidently and in Thanksgiving. Appreciating what God has Done, and to what's in-store. Because a Table is being prepared for My Now and My Forevermore. In order for you to Comprehend what I'm saying, you have to fully understand. That I'm not your imagination, I'm a Praying Man.

I'm not here to confront you, nor am I here for war. I'm just thanking our father, the one whom we adore. I'm not perfect by any means, nor I'm here for personal gain. Although we live different Lives, I share your Pain. Whether I went through it or shared other's experiences. I Pray that together we go to God, and get past our differences. I'm no better than you, you no better than me. But there's power in unity therefore we can succeed. In order for you to Comprehend what I'm saying, look at my Grasped Hands. I'm called Strength, I am a Praying Man.

I may not know your story, nor is it My Business. But I also pray to God for Yours and My Forgiveness. It's something that I've learned in this walk of life. That it's great to Pray For your strength through your strife. So, what I'm saying to you, is make your request Known and Clear. I go to God in Prayer every day of the Year.

In other words, I Pray without Ceasing. This enhances My Faith, which is God Pleasing. In order for you to Comprehend what I'm saying, let us join Hands. Then You'll Know and understand, that I'm a Praying Man.

From Conditioned to Commissioned

I'll Rise Above It All

Devil: Where are you going? I am your true friend. I was with you through the trials, I was there at the end.

Remember I was the one who said that I'll pray for you, even when the storms rage. I'm the one who told you stories to keep you engaged.

I'm the one who pointed out that you live among deceivers. I told you if you enter into that church it'll be filled with non-believers.

Now look at you, you basically have no place to go. But back to the way you were when money was in constant flow.

Life was easier when you were out in the world. You were the main man, everyone's favorite girl.

You had cars and houses in your possession. You even had bodyguards and guns as your secret weapons.

Yeah you say that no weapon formed against you will not prosper. But one bullet pierced your side and now no one wants to bother.

Because you started praising this God who asked for you to trust him. But since you made him your God, you're losing every game you used to win.

So why not stay with me, let me be your god. I'm the one who stopped you from going behind bars.

Stay with me, worship me, I am your friend. I Love you from head to toe, from beginning to end.

You: You do make a valid point, but I'm sorry I am a believer. Would you die for me or make me out to be the receiver?

The receiver of everyone's burdens, trials and tribulations. Or would you just want to rule over my life and all nations?

You were upset that you never got to sit on God's throne. Then try to make me give up the very blessing that God assigned for my own.

Yes, you were the friend that was in disguise. Milking every fiber of my soul waiting for my demise.

You did tell me that the church was filled with non-believers, but you lied. They were believers wanting to change, and have life no longer compromised.

They, like me, didn't want to live the life in which you've planned. They wanted to be someone who God created by being a Virtuous Woman, or a Kingdom Man.

We want to live and influence the work of God to all Nations. We also want to raise our Children to be a part of our Legacy Generation.

The money that I had in comparison to what's ahead is too small. Because I'm trusting on God who gave me the strength to rise above it all.

Dwayne J. Torres

King's Ransom

Devil: You are entrapped by the spirit of deceit, one more move and you'll be in defeat.

I have already outlined your grave. I am your Master and you are my Slave.

At the end of the day you'll bow down to me, for generations your family hung from a tree.

If you continue to get out of line, I'll show you who's boss. I even put the Son of God on the Cross.

In the darkest shadows I'm near you as a fright. When you look at your reflection, I am the darkness to your light.

You'll never live up to what is expected of you. Because there's no strength in all that you can do.

Look at you, you look like a fool, you think you sit on a throne when it's actually a stool.

Every time you thought you've won, in the end I make you lose. With that fear in your heart, that's no pick and choose.

You can't stop me because over you I live the superior. Do you think that Jesus is your real deliverer?

I'm immortal, look at the giant before you which he stands. You're the bug under my feet, you're a mere man.

Check your weather, I am your climate. I've closed your mind so you'll stay in your environment.

When it comes to the environment, my world is a team of expansion. You are nothing but little king and I am holding you at Ransom.

Me: I must be important to you that you want to hold me hostage. Which means that you're scared of me, while I continue to pay God Homage.

I like the silique, of the stool and the Throne. You obviously want me to switch, which is why you won't leave me alone.

I am King because God says I am. I am the heir to the throne, even though in flesh I am a Man.

You attack my mind hoping that I will dwindle. But as you can see devil, it's not that simple.

Because I am covered under the Blood. God raised that standard when you came in like a flood.

I am released from your bondage and my soul is set free. My sins are forgiven, and my mind is at ease.

You thought you won, but you forgot the cost. Jesus already gave me authority before he went to the cross.

So now look at you, your plans have been cancelled. God never gives me more than I can handle.

Which means if he gave me this fight, its already won. I never stepped in the ring, because God sent his only begotten Son.

You don't have me devil, so go ahead and take the Loss. Because My God, Jesus, and The Holy Spirit made me the boss.

Because he did not give me the spirit of fear, or life less defined. But the Spirit of Power, Love and a Sound Mind.

A Queen's Price

Devil: I told you to eat from the tree of life. I'm responsible for you not being a wife.

Look at you, a self-proclaimed Queen. Do you really believe that you are a Man's Dream?

Oh, I forgot you're not into them, you're too much into yourself. Trying to find Fame with superficial gods and unshared wealth.

You need makeup to cover your flaws. Standing at a closed door when your blessing is down the hall.

You walk slow so the men can watch your body. Then you deny yourself to their love because you're waiting on being a hotty.

Then you want to criticize other women who got it going on. Jealous of their clothes, jobs, man, and so on, and so on.

Then you act as if you deserve the best. Trying to keep up with the women on Love and Hip-Hop, your children thinks that you're a mess.

Stay in your lane woman, you don't have your priority straight. Even your girlfriend talks behind your back at an extreme rate.

Your man doesn't trust you, your daughter despises you. Your mother pities you, and your father doesn't even know you.

Your hair weave covers your naps and hair full of lice. Now kneel Before Me, it's time to pay the piper, you know the Price.

Now bow before me and serve me as your lord, because you know. You've already denied Jesus, you owe me your soul.

Woman: First and Foremost, I am not a Queen by self-proclaim. God told me that I am an Heir to his Throne, which means he knows my name.

I walk slow, not so much to get a man's attention. I walk with my head up with a lil sensual extension.

It's a Woman thing that you'll never understand. My Strength and Beauty Puts Fear in a Weak Man.

Speaking of weak devil, I'm talking about you. You're just mad because its God whom I choose.

You are such a liar, you seduce us with words of fakeness and flattery. You keep sending wolves disguised as sheep, then I have a case of Assault and Battery.

You've mistaken me with other women who sold their souls to you. Looking for love in wrong places along with a superficial attitude.

You fear me because I know my value and worth. I'm the most important Human Being on this Earth.

You display Jesters, Jezebels, Delilah's, Goliath's, to put me on a scale from 10 to Zero. But I'm the First Teacher, Nurturer, Preacher, Mother, Supreme Super Hero.

You cannot stop my Praise, because I'm covered under the blood. A Prophet told me that God raised the Standard when you came in like a Flood. So, the Standard was raised, and your flood has digressed. Now you want to start something, but I already passed the test.

Because I'm a woman who is Beautiful, Loved, with a purpose and a life. No longer will My Kingdom be in ransom, because this Queen has paid the price.

Be My Abel, Not My Cain

Say Brother, we don't have to compete. Especially when You and I Sit in the Same Seat.

We both are Broken, we both are Men. We learn to be independent, but we both are spent.

So why do we argue, why do we hate? We should support each other's kingdom, not fight or debate.

Oh, I see, you're too focused on my Territory. You want to be blessed like me, but don't want my story.

How can you live like me, when you don't want to go through? I'm sorry, you can't take what is mine, especially when you can't take my impurities or flu.

Understand what's mine was never designed for you to take. Because if you were to take it, it'll be your fatal mistake.

Because mine was consecrated By God and The Holy Spirit. Which means you can never have my life, or my blessings, period.

But I could see the knife in your hand, which clearly means that you don't understand.

That unless you have an alternate plan, you'll forever be living under my hand.

You may be able to steal, and you may take my life. But my legacy will forever be over your head, while you live in strife.

Because my blessing could never be yours, because it is my name on those doors.

So accept your favor and live throughout your pain.   Because your purpose is to be my Abel, not my Cain.

Come on brother, God has created you which means you're able. That you can live a life beyond, the Social Media Fable.

You have been equipped to be very successful. You don't have to look at my intangibles, and get all stressful.

You are wondering how I am able to relax, without liquor or weed. Because when it comes to tension, I get down on my knees.

Praying about my pain and for the oppressed. Then leaving it up to God, and living blessed.

You can live worry free if you believe. Then realizing that with God, there's nothing that you can't achieve.

God is greater than your mountains, can cover your sin. Jesus paid the price, all is forgiven.

Don't allow envy to become your crimson stain. You'll live in defeat, and hate is the only gain.

You can cross that river, or swim upstream. Be that Warrior and uplift your self-esteem.

You're a King, a Soldier, and a Warrior in Demand. When you're too Focused on My Kingdom, Yours will never stand.

You must protect your Queen from the Snakes in the Tree. You can never uphold your manhood by destroying me.

It'll alternate your journey to a path straight to hell. Which will only place your Queen and Kingdom inside of a Prison Cell.

When you go to jail, so does your woman and her soul. Because her spirit will fall without your heart to uphold.

So when I say let's speak peace and be grateful. I'm speaking of a brotherhood to live faithful.

Stand on your ground and look at your blessed table. Remember I am not your Cain, I am your Abel.

How Can You Judge Me?

How can you doubt me, because I didn't win Triumphantly? How can you see my way, when you don't live in This Biography?

You say that I'm great, but my reality is clear. When I speak of My Pain, you turn into a Deaf Ear.

You try to teach me, of how to Get Out of My Situation. But won't give me money for My Tuition, to Continue My Education.

You applaud my Efforts, but won't give me a Snack. Talk about me worse, than those Who Stab Me in The Back.

How Can You Judge Me, with very Little Evaluation? When I just heard you questioning God, about your Salvation?

Please don't think less of me, because I wasn't raised like you. Jesus was born in a Manger, But Wasn't Raised in A Zoo.

My clothes may be dirty, and my mind is cluttered. But even Moses lead his people, and he had a Stutter.

Oh, you didn't know that I know his word? Sure, I do, some of the best stories I've ever heard.

But that's not the only thing that keeps me going. Its literature is Full of Understanding, Knowledge in The Knowing.

They say never judge a book by Its cover. Because you never know who really lives Undercover.

Not every I is dotted, and every T is crossed. Not every master that Leads, is a True Boss.

My fantasy is your reality, Your Garbage, might be My Gold. But neither one of us, can Take nor Purify Souls.

Whether we live in a hut or a mansion, we all can succeed. God Gives Us Power, A Sound Mind, A Love Master's Degree.

Please don't Judge Me, especially when I don't see it your way. I'll reject your Chastisement, But Will Accept It If You Pray.

Because that will stir me to make the right decision. That'll lead us to a Priesthood Coalition.

We can break a curse of Many Generations. Start leading people to a Christ Dominion Nation.

Love starts with you; bound spirits are Set Free. When you take the Time to Pray, And Not Judge Me.

I Don't Mean to Get Political But...

Why Do You Call Me Nigger?

You use that word to describe My Great Grandfather, and My Ancestors.

Used that word so loosely that a book was written about it by a College Professor.

Are you intimidated by my build, or My Women's Figure?

Why is it that you call me a Nigger?

Is it a mind game because of its definition of ignorance?

Did you teach it to your child to destroy their innocence?

I Believe you use it to keep my mind enslaved.

Building Government Buildings on top of my Ancestor's Grave.

It was them that helped build this great land.

Then you want to Criticize My NFL Brothers because they won't stand.

Trust me, they love this Country as much as you do.

They are just tired of brutality from our Officers in Blue.

You use one of our own to say that slavery was a choice.

How can you agree with him, when you still don't listen to our voice?

Because when I speak it, you're saying that I'm being bitter?

Why is it that you call me a Nigger?

When you say the word, it's like venom flowing through my veins.

It kills my spirit, causing a generation a whole lot of pain.

So we took it back, but spelled as N-I-G-G-A.

Meaning, Non-Immigrants Gaining Gathering Achieving, is what Eddie Griffin say.

A Comedian whose words were so profound, reminding me that I will achieve on a higher ground.

Had a President whose skin was dark like mine. The Key of a Dream that was so Divine.

When he was Elected, there was a huge celebration. Noticing the change in this great nation.

However, he was slammed because he cared for the people. Seeing that every American Gets Health care as an equal.

Yet when all was said and done, we saw that his heart was bigger. But yet behind his back, you still called him a nigger.

We are more than athletes, we are more than lawyers. All we want to do, is create a legacy for our sons and daughters.

We are more than Rappers' hip-hopping our story. You Tie a noose around our necks, but yet we still give God the Glory.

We are More than Actors and Entertainers. When it comes to the beauty of this country, we're the original painters.

You say that we are a people, who look for handouts, Playing welfare games. Then Used certain Individuals, who don't even know their names.

They believe in a system that doesn't tell them who they really are. Not knowing that they are among the rising stars.

Some of us sold drugs to our community, a Neighborhood Suicide. Wanting to jack up the price of rent, so we could be victims of Societal Genocide.

We may talk with a slang, a swag in which you try to imitate. We are a people of Soul in which you can never duplicate.

But it's ok, we know who the real gangsta is. Learning of our Royalty is a Pop Quiz.

But One day you'll see, that you are no different from me.

I am human first, and yes Black Lives Matter. It should be a subject to all of the Congress Chatter.

Because if we all matter, You'll Heal the Misunderstanding. Allowing all of us Rising Together, While Love will be Expanding.

So Before You side with someone who pulled An Unnecessary Trigger. Ask Yourself, why did they call me a nigger?

I Am

You see me, and you've heard of my story. But some of my predecessors have me placed in a category. Most fear me, especially when Full of Knowledge. Which is why you want to place me in an uncredited Community College. I'm very athletic, and My Build is Strong. Even when overweight, I still turn Ladies On. They may not like me physically, but they fall in Love with my intellect. Reminding Them of Their Royalty, which I Vowed to Protect. Some see me as a brother, some see me as a threat. Some will praise my abilities, some will call me a suspect. I cannot speak of those before me, but I was born a Man. God allowed me to be a King, I am who God Says I am.

If you ever walk in My shoes, you'll know of the Battles I've Faced. You'll know that I'm not angry, although I've been disgraced. It's simply because of the color of My skin, or My Slang-ish Dialogue. I've come from a Family of Royalty, look at My Story Prologue. But if you get to know me, you'll see that I'm a cool guy. You'll want to be My Brother, not leave me to die. You'll want to help me build my community, and help me stand. God Made Me A Leader, I Am Who God Says I am.

Did you hear My Speeches, or admire My Achievements? Did you cover your eyes and ears when My People was going through Bereavement? Did You Aim at Me when I Began to Soar?

Did you realize, that it was I who held your door? Did you enjoy My show, did you think that I was funny? If you say in God we Trust, why do you withhold My Money?

I'm not here to beat you up, I just want to live. Love My Woman Right, and a Family Life to Give. Learn how I went from a Prince to a King. I Master My Professions, to the Third Degree. My People and I will Arrive to Our Promise Land. Because God Said it is So, I am Who God Says I Am.

Am I My Brother's Keeper?

Am I My Brother's Keeper? Yes, I am. I'm the demonstration of Help to My Fellow Man. Do I pray for all of the brothers? Of course I do. Because we have to lift each other up from the one Who Consumes. Our Mind Body and Soul. We can't allow Satan to take control. We have women on this Earth in whom we must protect. The First Teachers of our Nations, don't allow them to be a subject. A Subject of Low Esteem, and a Dependency Spirit. Uplift your Queens, by God's Love and Wisdom you inherit. Build up a Foundation, by investing upon good ground. Becoming Your Vision, while Heaven smile upon your Crown. Yes we are heavily criticized, and don't always get Acknowledged by Management. Because we're Born with Greatness from the Original Establishment.

We've measured our masculinity by what society and what other brothers say. Yet not realizing when we do, we cause our very own decay. God gave us power to Grow into a Phenom. Queens will Look at us like Adonis and Beyond. We have the capability to bring our Children Joy and Peace. By Being the assertive Figure while Goals Reaching its peak. We do have a competitive nature which makes us different. But we're the Kings of Society, our Women and Children are Dependent. So instead of destroying and coveting our neighbors' home, we need to stand and pray protecting our own. You are a Man of God, A King in your own right. Build your Kingdom, stand up and Fight. I Got Your Back from a Devil's Attack. We're the First Super Hero, our children look upon. Teach them to be Royalty, and not A Jester's Pawn. We have to get it together because the World is our Responsibility. Show your Queen that you'll master every opportunity. Because she'll follow, and Respect you with Love and Authority. Living life as Majesty should be your Top Priority. We Were Born to be as God Given Leaders. My Name is Dwayne, and I'm My Brother's Keeper.

Dear Democrats and Republicans

You love our country, but you all can't agree. You all are smart individuals, Some with a PHD.

You speak of togetherness, yet you're all far apart. Then some of you claim that you decide with your heart.

How can you say with your heart, when children and parents are being separated? Then you feel justified to do so, which no one has debated.

Accept money from corporations to help make your decision. Then say that every news reported about our President is mere superstition.

But yet he claims that he wants to make America Great Again. A country that has individuals who discriminate those of religion or the color of their skin.

This Country was Born of Slaves and partial Christianity. Vietnam Vets still trying to cope with life while fighting insanity.

Come on Parties, you know that you have to do better. Belittling those who disagree does not make you look any clever.

During our Pledge of Allegiance, we are one Nation under God. But yet, You Criticize the Less Fortunate, when their life is Hard.

You stand by and watch people grow hungry with no home to live. Thanksgiving and Christmas is the only time you give.

You destroyed the well fare system, why? Why you do not want your tax dollars to help? But yet Bail out Banks because they watch over your assets and wealth? I understand that you all disagree, but why so divided? Why do you allow the 99% to feel cheated and slighted?

Why are the tax breaks going to the wealthy and Corporations? And why do you allow FOX, & MSNBC News Speak Falsely Of our Nation?

Why are they so caught up to a One Sided Point of View? But yet never giving any Solutions to the Nation Problems or its Issues?

People are confused, and they don't know where to turn. You don't want to give Teachers a Reliable Salary for them to Earn.

Why isn't the Minimum Wage at $33.25? While making sure that your salary rises every day on the hive.

You say that Gays have no Rights, yet celebrate their pride. Then say they're living wrong, God is not on their side.

How can You say You Love God whom we cannot See? Yet hoarding on to Money like a Dam is to a Sea.

But who am I? I'm just a citizen who cares and loves the United States. Even though some of our leaders harbor, spit venom, and hate.

I can debate until my face is blue, we are supposed to be a United Nation that Stands True.

We can come Together when our soil is attacked, but why can't you all have our backs?

We vote for you believing in the change for the better, but you allow the corporate bucks to control your weather.

Listen, I'm not trying to be harsh nor lame, I just need for both parties to explain.

Why can't we agree and take care of our own, and leave our parties selfishness alone?

Give back to those who are in need, invest in our education so our children could succeed.

Open the Doors to Those who is yearning to be free, No one can take away our national creed.

We hold these truths to be self-evident, let's create an environment

where we could love and repent. You are my Brother/Sister we are one Nation, we should raise awareness for the next generation.

So they can excel and learn from our mistakes, which should be a priority whatever it takes.

I still believe in the country, despite disagreeing with some of its leaders. Some of us just need a breather.

Dwayne J. Torres

Kanye's Prayer

Kanye: Dear God, I am in tears wondering why I betrayed my peers. I'm searching for myself even though I'm deep into my mental illness, where people are questioning if I'm the realist. I only support Donald Trump to express my freedom of speech, but my soul is drowning so far, that it's hard to reach. I claimed that Bush doesn't care about my people, and now I feel like I called the ghetto black, and they look at me like I'm evil. How can I reach my hand out to you when I made Jesus walks, but the devil whispers in my ear when I talk? Explain to me father, if I can stretch my hand to you I can see. I am in the sunken place where I just need to be free. From politics and my wife being called a whore, where I can't even wipe the blood from my ancestors backs off the white man's floors. I seek for guidance, but you took my mother away.

I was a loose cannon when she was around, and she still stayed and prayed. I lost my faith within my Godly form and took it as Yeezus. How can I claim myself as God when I'm not close to Jesus? I made enemies that was unnecessary from the start. With Jay Z I shared my fame & glory and I tore it apart. So please show me the error of my ways and I'll be here to pray always.

God: Kanye West I'm not angry with you, but disappointed in what you've become. You spoke for your people and sold your soul to give a white man a gun. To continue to destroy my children without warning. To a president who doesn't even believe in global warming. I still love you because I can still see greatness within your heart. You can't make America great again if you can't be

57

smart. Teach others on how to stand in dark days. I'm watching all movement, even demons hiding in shades. Darkness may surround you, but I taught you better. You rebuke the flesh like holy water, within every drop I am greater. Change your image and realize you are blessed. Forgive yourself first, and release the stress. Stop carrying the world around your shoulders, and allow people to see you through me. Because I don't have to brag, I can make a demon bleed.

Your sins are forgiven in my eyes if you call my name. Don't say slavery was a choice, when Moses had to fight for the promise land, and his enemies was sent to shame. I'm the leader of this order, even when the devil may think he's won. But I will always defeat him, and love you because you are my son. Change your spirit around the choices you make, because if you don't choose me the wickedness will take. Realize who you are before it's too late. If you don't fight for what's right, your soul will break. I still have faith in you Mr. West, but I'm always watching you, so pass the next test.

- Dwayne Torres II

Foundation

Jesus

You Rose from the dead, you are the reason that I have daily bread.

You are the receiver of my sins, you made sure that I don't play the game of life to win.

I play to arrive, to reach the peak of my soul, and my spirit purified.

You didn't allow me to give up my talents, just so I can please man.

You had me trade in my talents and be about God's plan.

You want me to succeed in all that I do. You chastise me when I don't speak the truth.

You told me to trust your Father who art in Heaven. Who is the Keeper of my soul, and you blessed it.

I cannot thank you enough for what you did for me.

You asked for my forgiveness, so I can live free.

Jesus, you are my all in all.

Always catch me when I fall.

You cleared my eyes, so I can see.

You're always talking to God, you Intercede.

You pray for my life in which I don't deserve.

Which is why for you I live and serve.

Thank you, for never forsaking and believing in me, in you and God I trust.

Thank you, Father God, for giving us your Son, Jesus.

Know Your Authority, By Learning My Story

Jesus: If you have a minute, I want to tell you a story. About how I became me and have given you authority.

I was born in a manger, I had on swaddling clothes. Even as a baby, I had an insecure King as my foe.

He sent wise men to spy and have me killed. Which would've given the devil such a thrill.

He celebrated sin, like it was a parade. He wanted me to stop, but my timing was not delayed.

But I was sent to give you life. To be a remembrance, when you go through strife.

I've fed 5,000 and I've made the blind see. I've walked on water, Cured many Disease.

I talk with a diction, and I tell many parables. True stories to Heart and noting imaginable.

I tell God about you, especially if you believe. I've asked God to forgive you, even when you deceive.

I calm the storms, while religious leaders had a debate. Even a Centurion who heard of me, had a lot of faith.

Because he believed in my words, as well as to who I am. My Disciples, called me The Christ, and became Fishers of Man.

I came to give you life and give it more abundantly. So listen while I tell you about your authority.

I told a tree that it'll never grow, I said that you'll do greater things. Just listen how I flowed.

I asked God to forgive you of all of your sins. Whenever the devil wants to fight, I make sure that you win.

Realize that every battle you face, it's not yours it's mine. I want you to remember that I overcame the world of all mankind.

I am the peace when you start to worry. The setbacks that come, is only Temporary.

You see My Brother/Sister you can move mountains, with a faith of a very tiny seed. You have to understand the power of Declaring and Decreeing.

Your tongue has the power to build or destroy. Your discerning spirit will show you who's the real McCoy.

I was given all power before I was ascended To Heaven. One of My Disciples betrayed me, which is why I was left with Eleven.

But I forgave him, but that was something he never knew. Just like all of your sins, I've asked God to Forgive you.

So now that you know about me and my story. Go ahead and read the Gospels, and learn more about each life's category.

When you find out why I did it, You'll Give God the Glory. Now walk with your heads up, and walk with Authority.

Inspirationally Redeemed

When I Arrived

I was on this Journey, I heard about My Friend. Many has told me that his life is coming to an end. But I didn't Fret, Nor Did I Worry. Because I knew I'll be Spiritually Operating, in a new Territory. And That is Speaking Life to the Dead. Show the Multitude of Faith, over Worry Instead. When you speak Life, More Doors are Opened. Because it lifts the heavy laden, and fixes the Broken. When I arrived, I was told that my friend had passed away. He'd still be living if you had come, and Not been Delayed. I felt their pain, so I'd shed some Tears. Because at that moment, I understood their Fears. So I walked towards the Tomb, stretched My Hand and Shout. Lazarus Come Out.

He walked out wrapped up in Grave Clothes. Amazingly he wasn't eaten by maggots or decomposed. He walked out of the Sepulcher Willing and Hungry. I wanted to see him Liberated and Become Free. It's a New Chapter Right Now, a New Season is Dawning. Awaken Your Spirit, I know you're tired, that's why you're yawning.

Your Promise is Not Dead, nor is it in Hibernation. You are the Leader to Your Legacy Generation. I heard your prayers and I've Blessed Your Tears. The Promise has broken ground, it started Construction This Year. Last year was your blue print, your faith is your contract of action. The only fine print is don't allow any more distractions. You have this Gift, and I want you to Bless the World.

Let it Heal, let it Unfurl. Your enemies will be in disbelief, when they see how your Soul Survives. Demons will Flee, doubts will be Destroyed, All Things New, When I Arrive.

There's Got To be A Cross For Me

I see you Jesus, you sacrifice for me. You Saved My Soul, so I could Live Free. You've broken generational curses, and Religious Traditions. Dying for me on The Cross was a Very Tough decision. But you've done it, nonetheless. Then you Spoke to God, declared Me Blessed. Which means that You Truly Love us and Care. Which also means that I will also have a cross to Bare. Although it's heavy, I'm able to carry it through. You've Risen on the Third Day, Life's Best Ever News.

I've walked through the Valley of the Shadow of Death. I did forget about the Promises you've kept. Which is why the Cross felt heavier than it seemed. Fighting off demons who try to kill My Esteem. Talking about how I'll never be a part of God's Plan. Even if I repent, I'll never make it to The Promise Land. But the Devil is a Liar, I'm a part of a Royal Priesthood. Everything will work Together for My Good. If I should ever fall, My Cross will then get lifted. By the Assist of God, Jesus, and the Holy Spirit. Who'll act together as one. That's when I realized My New Life Has Begun. Because Jesus Bared The Cross, but he wasn't alone. He did it for Love and to have my Sins Atoned. Thank You Jesus for making me Free. Because now I understand... There's Got To be A Cross for Me.

My Earnest Prayer

My Gracious Heavenly Father, in the Mighty Name of Jesus. Thank You for being our Father, when many Leave Us. I Thank you for hearing me as I Pray, For Tonight I'm Giving Myself Away. I've taken My Life for Granted not realizing. That your ways are directing me to My Purpose, so I'm standing here Apologizing. That I tried to do this on my own, and yet I've always failed. Because I didn't want to be patient, and I felt like you've bailed. Now I want to take Responsibility for My Actions, and Lord I want to Repent. I look back and see how much wasted time I've spent. Trying to impress those who was not for me, while I treat those in my corner wrong. Trying to fit into a Crowd of people where I Don't Belong.

But I woke up this morning wanting a change. Fix My Heart Lord, so My Soul Could be Rearranged. Breathe Life into Me and fix this broken vessel. I apologize for playing games with the devil. Father can you hear me now? I'm looking towards the sky. I'm calling out to you while throwing away My Pride.

You've heard me Lord, you've heard Me. You said in your word that I'll succeed. It's not about the Earthly Materialistic world that I'll achieve. But you have many Mansions assigned, yes Lord I Believe. I saw Jesus's Nail Prints and Now I Understand. That if we trust you, we'll see that Your Blessings are On Demand. Thank You So Much Father, For Giving Me My Faith's Lesson. I'm going to My Warehouse and retrieve All of My Blessings. You are truly My Father and I'm Forever Grateful To you. Saturate Me with Your Anointing like Sweet Morning Dew.

Thank you again Father God, for Always Being There. Thank You for Listening, Hearing, and Answering My Earnest Prayer. In Jesus Name I Pray, Amen, Amen, and Amen.

Love

I Want to Be Your Man

I don't know you, but I want to. I want to make you proud of the Queen that's inside of you.

Because of that Queen, I was able to recognize your Beauty and Royalty. Knowing of your worth and living under God's Authority.

Have you ever had a man pray for you who wasn't family? If so, did he speak to God with Praise and Charity?

If not it's ok, because I want you to know why he didn't. Because God was waiting for me to show you that a good man existed.

No, I am not perfect, yes, I do have some flaws. But I'm the one with chivalry and holding your opened doors.

The Skeletons in your closet, I am not afraid of them. Let's just move forward and let our new life begin.

They may fall out and put others in fear. But I'm commissioned to be your covering, and I'll still call you My Baby, My Dear.

I know that I may come off a lil over confident. But it's ok because if you take a piece of my Love it'll become evident.

That I'm here to lead you to a place in his Kingdom. Which is why I pray over your Spirit and Ask God to give you Wisdom.

I want you to see me through Kingdom and Virtuous Eyes. I don't have any hidden agenda, I don't want your life compromised.

I want to introduce you to the God in me. See for yourself, as I make this clarity.

I am the one who has visions and plans. What I'm really trying to say is, that I want to be your man.

Lead you to a Kingdom where God is praised, who will never forsake you or go astray. You're worth every effort that I could ever make. Praying to God for you not for sexual but for Love's sake.

I'm making this very clear, as I stand before you. With God on our side, I'll commit to keep you smiling when you're blue. I want to be the Man that you dream of. I want to be the King that you fall In Love.

With these open arms, I want you to understand. That today and every day, I want to be your man.

Is This Love?

Man: I know a man ain't supposed to cry. But I'm going to let these tears flow from my eyes.

Because I am Blessed, by God whom never gave me short of his Best.

I had my share of women, who were the desires of my daydreams. But God placed them all together in My Beautiful Nubian Queen.

Skin Silky soft of Ebony, a Vocabulary of a Professor. Love the King in me, while sending away her Jesters.

She encourages me to reach beyond any measures. She doesn't see serving me as a chore, she sees it as a pleasure.

Because she doesn't serve me as master to a slave. She Serves with her Royalty, My Crown in her engraved.

She compliments Me, and My Debonair Swag. She's Loyalty Walking, not Labeled or Tagged.

She moves with a sexy walk of a movie in slow motion. Never stops being a Queen while giving me her Devotion.

She's the Woman that your mother will come to love and appreciate. Because she has the quality of a Queen that makes this King Celebrate.

I am her Soaring Eagle, she's My Flying Dove. I'll never have to ask, is this Love?

Woman: I wasn't a Damsel in Distress, but you've rescued me. From believing that I'm not worthy, you've elevated my esteem.

I've cherished every moment, whenever I'm with you. You help me look at my life from a different point of view.

Realizing that I'm a Queen separated from the World. Humbled, Grateful, Honored, with the Heart of a Little Girl.

Not to the point of immatureness where I allow a jester to have his way. I have been transformed by God, I start a New Life Every day.

You came into my life, and reminded me of my Royalty. Which is why I don't mind serving you, with Love and Loyalty.

You've shown me Real Love, and that My King still existed. You've been honest with me in actions, and don't have my mind twisted.

I don't have to guess nor question God above. I've been blessed with a King, yes, this is Love.

My Forever Ride Or Die

Male: Ride or Die is a slogan most people use. But not everyone understands the Soliloquy, so it's sometimes misused.

But What it's truly saying, is that can you stand the rain? And Will you be able to withstand, My Joy or My Pain?

Can you match my crazy or my insane? Or Can you still love me whether I Lose or Gain?

My Kingdom is always at war, will you be there? If I Fall Will you Catch Me, or Would you Even Care?

Realize That you Have to Be My Bonnie To My Clyde. Love Me Whether I'm Dr. Jekyll or Mr. Hyde.

If You Can say Yes, then I'll know that I'm Blessed.

Because I am Right Here Not Trying to Hide. Thank You Love for Forever Being My Ride or Die.

Female: I don't know as to whom you had before, but I ain't the one. I've been designed to be your Queen since my Life begun.

It's funny I did not feel this way with no other man. I guess you were my assignment, it was you all along within God's plan.

You see the ones before me couldn't develop such a love. Because they were your Ravens and I am your Dove.

You came at me with a Dr. Jekyll Smile, but Your Hyde was your Pride. You allowed my spirit to reach you, which is why I became your bride.

Which means I'm not scared of you, nor would I turn my back. Would stand in the gap for you, from every demonic attack.

You see there's no need for me to climb mountains, nor swim the deep seas. I am the Umbrella to your soul, I am the one with whom you're pleased.

But don't misuse my love because another wants to take my place. You'll find out that she's not your lady, but I am your grace.

So if you take a look, and study my stride. You'll know that I'm Forever Your Ride or Die.

My Very Best Friend

Woman: You came into my life, when I was Broken. Because too many words were clearly Unspoken. A Suspicion, that caused me to question My Own Ability. My Self Worth, Not knowing My Own Liberty. But what I found in you, helped me realize My Worth. Reminded me that I have Purpose on This Earth. Can't explain why it took you for me to see it. So many blessings are Available for Me to Receive It. You were a part of a chapter that was written. Of my story which I thought my Life Was Intermittent. I forgot that God knows My Beginning, and My End. He Gave Me Life, He Gave Me You, My Very Best Friend.

Man: I never understood my purpose until I met you. I saw My Clouds, but you saw My Skies Blue. I allowed my Idiosyncrasies, to blind me, of My Worth. Forgetting Royalty was upon me Since My Day of Birth. When speaking life, you told me to Believe in It. Validating God's words Promises of Achieving It. I should've believed God when he told me of My Land of Promise. Where your love dwelled, so alluring & honest. Jesus authors our Faith from Beginning to End. Thank you Beautiful for Being My Very Best Friend.

Together: God Assigned You to Me, So That I Could See. The

Beauty of His Glory, And His Blessings Exclusively. I Had an Idea, But You've Proved Me Wrong. I Was Always Meant to Sing, Our Soul's Song. With You I've Found the Right Tune, As We Sing in Harmony. Growing Together in Christ, While Never Singing Off Key. If My Story Ends Today, I Could Say That I've Lived. I'm Not

Subjected to Fear, Only the Power That God Gives. So Tonight, As I End My Prayers with Love And Amen. I Want to Stop and say Thank You For Being My Very Best Friend.

My Queen

Although I was awake, I thought it was a dream. You were the sight of beauty with a Royalty Esteem. There was something about you, that I wanted to get to know. Yes, I admired your body, but prayed for a Righteous Soul. We all come short of His Glory. But your Virtuousness and Intellect, told Another Story. My prayers were answered, my love life fulfilled. My best foot forward, while my Pride Stood Still. Brokenness tried to stop you, but you Reign Victorious. You relied on The Holy Spirit, while Living Glorious. You empower those around you, you're a Love Supreme. I am Blessed, to call you My Alluring Queen.

There's no particular reason, or a Special Occasion. I just wanted to express, My Love and Appreciation. My world has changed since you've graced My Life. The epitome of beauty, who is my Partner, My Wife. My goal was to lift you up, and make your heart sing. While Giving God Glory, for being Your King. Our journeys were different, but have a common goal. Knowing that Victory is Inevitable, because God is in Control. I wanted you to live complete, while the devil lives in envy. God made you for me, My Beautiful Nubian Queen.

Waking Up in My Prayers

Man: I heard about God's Grace. So I wanted to seek his Face. I knew that I had sinned and come short of his glory. But I wanted My Life, to speak a different Story. In order for me to be what you need, I had to become the root of a dead seed. A seed that was planted on Good Ground. Growing Solidly into a Man of God, with a message so Profound. So I got on My knees and started to pray. And asked God how to Love, in a new way. He placed me here in your life for a reason. Either to be your Blessing, or be your season. I've asked God To be your Blessing. Although I also wanted to be your Lesson. So you can see what Real Love is supposed to be. So you are no longer bound in your past, and Live Free. I just want to show you that I Love You and I care. Feel My Soul, By Waking Up in My Prayers.

Woman: Oh Man of God, Your Love and Your Words are so Profound. Which is why I'm glad to wear that Bridal Gown. When My Heart went Broken, you placed it back together. Then you looked into My Eyes and said I'm here Forever. My past has taught me what I was missing. That true love comes in a form of Thanksgiving. Yes, I was hesitant because I didn't believe that you existed. Because men came as Kings, but really a Jester Twisted. So why did I surrender to your Love? Because you Lifted My Spirit, by praying to God Above. Not only you've shown me that you're a Warrior, you also speak life. Given God Praises and Elevation is what a man brings to a wife.

I'm so proud, oh yes I am. That God has Blessed me with a King as My Man. Your presence of Love is like a Breath of Fresh Air. Feel My Soul, when you wake up in My Prayers.

Inspired by God, an Agape Love

Dwayne J. Torres

When I Met Eve

Adam: I was a Man who was one with God. To you it may seem kind of Odd. That God had me name all of the Things on this Earth. A Bird, A Tree, even Gold Before I knew its Worth. It didn't have any worth because everything was equal. This was the life, during Sin's Prequel. I basically had everything all together. But God saw fit that I shouldn't be Alone Forever. He placed me asleep, took a part of My Rib. I've trusted My God, I knew that he wouldn't forbid. At that time, I was Learning about Love Not sin. Even though I had no competition, I was still hoping I'd win. Waking up to see another Life to Begin. When I opened My Eyes, Wow! God Created Woman. I was taken aback because I never saw such Beauty. Naming Her was another part of my duty. She stood and Looked so Beautifully Designed. I'm amazed that God Made her My Responsibility and Assigned. She's More to me than I've ever known. Together we're Born Fully Grown. Love was one of the First of Man to Achieve. She's the Tender Roni, upon My Esteem.

She's the First Helpmate Known to Man. The Mother of All Things of Love and Human. She's the First Virtuous Woman, The First Queen. Way Before Royalty even had a Meaning. She was the Mistress of Ceremony, The Star of the Show. She's one of the Teachers of Love, and how it flows. She's the Making of a Good Woman, before Sins stole her identity. Seduction had raped her, and the world lost its Beauty. Even though I've blamed her for My and Earth's Downfall, she remained confident, in control, and stood tall.

Still had My Back despite of our sins. She still wanted me to Achieve and to start Again. Yes, I'm amazed how in me she still believed. All of this happened the day I've met Eve.

My Answered Consecrated Prayer

Husband: I Pray for You, because I've asked God for a wife. I Pray for You Because You're the Deliverer of Life. I Pray for you, Because You're My Earth. I Pray for You Because I Know Your Worth. I Pray for you Because you're My Foundation. I Pray for you Because you're the Mother of our Nation. I Pray for you Because you're The Answer. To a Prayer to God, Our Given Soul Enhancer. I Pray for you Because of Love. I Pray for you Because I've Placed No One Else Above. I Pray for you Because God's Given My Heart's Desire. I Pray for you Because God made Me Your Required. Because He's Blessed Me with You, and The Love That We Share. I Thank God Because You're My Answered Consecrated Prayer.

Wife: I Pray for you Because I've asked God for a Husband. I Pray for you Because you're That Man. Who Faced the Trials and Tribulations that we came up Against. Who's My Strong Tower, Victorious over the Evil Prince. I Pray for you Because You've made My Heart Sing. I Pray for you Because you're My Soul Praying King. I Pray for you Because You Brought Laughter in My Sorrows. I Pray for you Because you're My Forever Tomorrow. I Pray for you Because You've Understood. What it takes to Love Like a Man of God Should. I Pray for You My King of Debonair. I Thank God for Blessing me with My Answered Consecrated Prayer.

Her Love Heals Me

Virtuously Made, a Woman of Valor. Her Botanical Gardens of Beautiful Flowers. When She Prays, My Demons Flee. She's Not Superficial, She Loves Me. Her Voice is Beautiful, soft and sweet. Her Love Brings Back, My Heart's missing Piece. I'm not perfect, but she doesn't Judge. Storms hit her home, and it never budged. Because she brings a foundation, along with her Spirit. If you want peace, she asks God to deliver It. Because she's with Purpose, who Genuinely Cares. She's Proverbs 31, No other Woman can Compare. Her Mission in Life is a Devil's Defeat. A Virtuous Wife, Her Mission's Complete.

So why do you seem so very adamant? Because I wanted to pay her a Beautiful Compliment. Why do you Love and Even Care? Because She's the Answer to My Consecrated Prayer. What Does she see in You? A Virtuous King Who Vowed I Do. That's Nice, but does she Know about Your Past? She Didn't Care, that's why we'll Forever Last. What about your sins of yesterday and today? She asked God to Forgive herself and I whenever she Prays. So what is it that you're confessing? That she's My Queen and My Blessing. So she's your perfect cup of tea? She's the Very Thought to My Daydream. She knows Jesus as The True Vine. She's God's Favor and My Assigned. She's Beautiful, has Wisdom, a woman with Honor. I Pray for God's Anointing Fall Fresh Upon Her. She's My Numbers after A to Z. Bless Her Heart, she's Love's Infinity. She Nurtures My Soul, with intimacy and Dignity. I'm Eternally Grateful, For Her Love Heals Me.

Inspired by Love, My Queen, and Proverbs 31

I'm Your Covering

I was born for a greater purpose. Like a Police Officer to serve and Protect. A job I gladly accept, and vowed to Never Neglect. My Mission is simple, yet difficult because of its service. A mission to deliver while standing and hovering. I am wonderfully made, powerfully displayed, you're made for me, I'm Your Covering. A Kingdom Man outside, True Warrior deep down. I sometimes walk with a frown, not because of tradition, because of my mission. To protect you from jesters and clowns. They come in like the devil in a flood. Waving their deceptions, by using sweet words as weapons. While sniffing out for Blood. But never worry what they try to do. For them it's a thrill, while try to hunt what they can't kill, fearing because I'm the real deal. Forever Loving and Covering You. I Love, and Respect you with every measure. Leading you to your aspirations, with Love and Determination. Your value and worth I'll always Treasure. Either I stand in front or have my wings and armor hovering. I am what you need, oh you better believe. I answered to God yes, he's given you the best. We will walk as Blessed even through storms and mess. My Mission is to please, and protect by all means. I am your King not your waiter, although I serve but for something greater. I am Forever in Gratitude Forever Loving You, I'm Your Covering.

Too Equipped to Quit

Dwayne J. Torres

When I Exceed Your Expectations

My Parents Had an Idea, But They Had No Clue. My Purpose Is from God, Not from Them or You. You Shouldn't Place A Cap on My Wisdom and Education. Because I Will Always Exceed Yours and My Expectations. Why Should I Measure Myself, By Yours and Societal Worth? Especially When Neither One of Us, Has Created This Beautiful Earth. When I Make A Statement, I Try to Make It Clear. When I Exceed Your Expectations, You Go from Praise to Fear. My Blessings Are Never Greater Than Yours. Focus on Your Craft, and Realize Your Blessed Doors. The Problem Is, You're Thinking That I'm on a Higher Level. I Just Kept Moving Forward, Not Stagnated by a Procrastinating Devil. Who Always Try to Deteriorate My Soul, Objectives, and Purpose. So I Stopped Believing in and Watching Our Societal Social Media Circus.

Please Don't Think That I'm Going to Stop, Because I've Grown to Know My Light. You're More Than Welcome to Some Shades, I Plan to Keep It Bright. I Understand That Sometimes, We've Looked at others With Envy. Disagreeing with Their Lifestyle, but wanting Their Merchants of Green. We Watch Them Rise, While Attracted to Their Greed. But We Don't Know How Many Times They Fell, or When They Bleed. But It's Not Our Job to Know, How and Why. Just Utilize Our Eagle Wings to Soar and Fly. I'm Still Not Where I Want to Be, Because I'm Still Growing. I've Decided to Wake Up My Ambitions and Keep 'Em From Snoring. Don't Be Like Cain, Murdering My Life Before My Destinations.

Inspirationally Redeemed

You Can Move Ahead, While Defeating Your Hesitations. Put Aside Your Pride and Resist All Temptations. Because My Legacy Will Remain, When I Exceed Your Expectations.

Dwayne J. Torres

Snakes In My Lawn

I hear them Hissing, but I cannot See Them.
They slither around My Atmosphere, discomforting My Equilibrium.
They Camouflage their Appearance, their Eyes are Hypnotizing.
Then later I wonder why, my goals are Compromising. It's Because
They are Great, at Their Craft. Some are a part of a Demonic Staff.
Punching in a Time Clock, Assigned for Your Demise. Waiting
Patiently, To Catch You by Surprise. They're not always Your
Enemies, they're disguised as Family and Friends. They May Even
Be Your Seed, Your Next of Kin. They Rattle their Tails, or Spit in
Your Eyes. They Suffocate Your Body, Their Venom is Suicide. They
invade Your Space, From Dusk to Dawn. Why Didn't I Kill the Snakes
in My Lawn?

I Didn't Kill Them, because That's Not My Nature. However, I'll Keep
an Eye on Them, watching Their Behavior. God already raised The
Standard, because they were flowing like a Flood. But too weak to
Strike, because they came Through The Blood. The Blood works, it
Forgives and Protects. Which is why they left My Lawn, a war
they'll never Forget. Left wondering, why I never stepped into The
Ring. Because God said, it's not My Battle, For Me to Bring. I did
Bring My Sword and Shield, but I didn't use them. Because Jesus's
Blood was so powerful, Their Hate Skewed Them. Don't complain,
don't let them Ruin Your Day. They'll realize Their Error, all you
have to do is Pray. If they call You Mr./Ms. Goodie Two Shoe,
touché. Because a Winter's Cold Will Never Understand, The Month
of May. You're the Rock/Peace of This Earth. Snakes want You to
Crawl, because they want Your Worth.

You're the King/Queen of Your Kingdom, and they're Just a Pawn.
You're the Master of Your Royalty, No More Snakes in Our Lawn.

Dwayne J. Torres

My Tears, My Story, My Victory

You see the Tracks, because it speaks. My Scars are real, sometimes My Blood Leaks. But it doesn't speak of what you see. It has a story that you'll not Believe. When it tells its story, it's beyond your imagination. Which is why I speak with a Lil hesitation. Like how I can still stand and say that I Forgive? Because Ezekiel Prophesied for My Dry Bones to Live. So when you see the tears on My Face, it's because I went from the Grave to Grace. When I woke up, I was Ready for War. I have new strength like never before. Someday you'll understand My Soul Surviving History. My Tears, My Story, My Victory.

Many Soldiers Ripped up My Body, left me for Dead. They never noticed the light upon my head. They were too busy wanting the Kill. High Five the Devil whom they thought was a thrill. But they've killed My Flesh, Not My Soul. God let them know that he's in control. So like Lazarus, I woke up Hungry. For the Word of God, then Continued My Journey. I'm so driven like a storm is to the seas. This is My Tears, My Story, My Victory.

I told you that you wouldn't Believe My Story. But I'll purposely wait for your testimony. Because once you're placed on that Battlefield, God's word becomes your sword and shield. Don't worry, you will survive. That's when you realize it's all a Blessing in Disguise. Because the Battle was never yours to begin with. Distractions are nothing but a mind drift. Drifting to a place called mislead. And you'll meet the same demons, who left me for Dead. Like me you're a Warrior of Faith and Power.

It started when you prayed in the Midnight Hour. You and I are equipped to solve our own Mysteries. Welcome to My Tears, My Story, My Victory.

My Promise is Purposed

Me: You've given Me a Life, That I've come to Know. Where you introduced Me to Jesus, and Love Overflow. Although I've asked, I've never felt like I deserved another Chance. Missing out on Grace, and Mercy from Your Blessed Hands. But Somehow you said that I was worthy. No Longer will I have to live in Hunger or Be Thirsty. But I Hunger for you, yet I still do wrong. You said it's a part of My process, just be strong. Because the pain I've received is not self-inflicted. My flesh gets weak therefore I get tempted. But Nevertheless, My Promise will Exceed. Because it's been Declared and Decreed. Thank You Father God, that My insecurities have been Reversed. Glory to God, My Promise Is Purposed.

God: My Precious Child, there's Reasons for the Process. So you can see and learn of your Promise. Each Rising Level Reached, came with a Test. Which is why The Devil always start Some Mess. Because he knows each level is a major threat. To his kingdom and satanic progress. You see, I've already ordered your steps. Each Movement can be a lil complex. But you'll make it to your Promised Border. You'll travel through Blessed Waters. High Tide or Low, your Blessing will overflow. It's not that you did any Good, or because you're deserving. It's because I made a Promise to you when Life was unnerving. My words never come back, nor have I've changed My Mind. Because I've Broken the Mole when creating Mankind. So yes, My Child, it's already been Declared and Decreed. I'm giving it to you exceedingly and abundantly.

All demonic residues have been Reversed. Yes, My Precious Child, Your Promise is Purposed.

Inspired by God, and His Promises. I'm Blessed and So are You. Be Blessed and Be a Blessing.

Dwayne J. Torres

I Got You

King: I've seen your distractions, but I want your focus. I'm trying to save you, from a Demonic locust. With the God in Me, My Love purifies. You'll be locust free in no time. The distractions are there, but not for your uplifting. Their Love is like magic, it keeps disappearing. They try to tame you like a Lion in a Circus. Making you Believe that they're there, for your purpose. If they were your purpose, you wouldn't need to be tamed. They'll Respect who you are, and get to know your name. Your name is Beautiful, Alluring, Phenomenally, Goddess, and Queen. You are a Virtuous Woman a Real King's Dream.

Allow the God in me to lead you, please take My Hand. I'll Move You from Your Egypt into Your Promise Land. Then You'll see that I'm a King, by the mighty God I serve. He Led Me to You, to be the Man you need and Deserve. I know that others said the same and it's hard for you to trust. It starts out beautifully then it turns into Lust. I'm not trying to convince you, I've Prayed that you'll see in Faith. That I'm here to Love and Protect you, Our Future Looks Great. There's no need to worry, let's you and I Pray. Then You'll see truth into the words that I say. I'm not here to tame nor control, But I'll Support Your Career. Talk to God for yourself, and he'll show you that I'm Sincere. I'll hold your hand while your heart heals. Then I'll let My Love show you, that I'm for real. A King is who I am, Love is what I do. Feel the intertwining of our Souls, and you'll see that I Got You.

Inspired by King's Honoring and Love Their Queen. Showing Your Princesses on how their Prince should Love and Protect Them.

You're Worth It

To My Little Queens

You were placed on This Earth, to be A Blessing to all. Which is why, The Devil Celebrates When You Fall. Young men came into your lives But Do They Realize Their Crowns? Do they celebrate their Royalty or Their World Around? Regardless of their answers, My Crown was placed on My Head. To Protect My Little Queens, a Daddy's Love Daily Bread. You are growing up before My Very Eyes. Hoping that you'll keep yours On the Prize. Because You're Heirs to His Throne. Seats and Designed by God who is God Alone. You Are the Epitome of a Young Lady. Don't Allow Social Media Make You Believe Maybe. Never allow Society to Dictate Who You Are. Because They Have No Idea of Your Journey or How Far. A Statement was made when you were Born. Sometimes your Heart May Get Torn. But you have a Father who is an Earthly King. Who Praises God, and loves his Royal Family, above any Materialistic Thing. Besides Your mother, you all are The Reality of My Dream. Being married to Her, and Raising Little Queens.

Each day I look at our Family, and I see That I'm Wealthy. By Our Father Above, a Love That's Blessed and Healthy. I've Raised and am raising Strong Little Kings and Queens. Grown and Growing to Live While Swimming Up Stream. I Thank God for you and our Lives Together. Some of You Moved Away, But Our Bond is Forever. Thank you, My Queen, for giving me Such Beautiful Angels. Nothing could ever Separate Us, Despite Life Changes. Cumi, Mon-Mon, Lili. Daddy Loves You Totally Completely.

Always Daddy's Little Girl. More Precious Than Any Diamond or Pearl. Reality Dreams, My Little Queens.

I'm Praying For You

I'm not here to Judge You, we just Live Differently. I want You to Survive, and Live in an Expectancy. There's Greatness in You, That's Greater Than the World. You are God's Precious Child, in his Arms we've Curled. Sometimes You Forget Your Purpose, Because of Distractions. The World Makes a Good Impression, but never leads to Satisfaction. It's a known fact that you Can Be Copied, but not Duplicated. Because you're Uniquely Made, you should be Celebrated. Which is why I'm on My Knees, and Praying to God for This Decree. I don't care What You Say or What You Do. I'm Calling out to God, and I'm Praying for You.

So What if I Don't know You, but I am Your Brother. I pray for your mind to be free, from worry and Clutter. Don't allow society to dictate your living and Keep you Shallow. You are Priceless, which means You're too high in Value. We are Heirs to His Throne, You're a Part of a Royal Priesthood. Which means We're Royalty Who Live in the Same Spiritual Neighborhood. The Jesus in Me Loves the Jesus in You. I'm Calling out to God, and I'm Praying for You.
I'm Praying for your Heart's Desire, moreover I'm Praying for His Will. We're forever in his Debt, but Jesus's Blood Paid the Bill. I Understand you've sinned, but we all fall Short. I'm Praying for You to Be Focused, not Your Vision Distort. Remember this, when you're weary and can't sleep at night. Me and My Prayer Partners, are sending Many Demons to Flight. When we pray, we Mention You by Name. Precious, his Child, not Your Sin, or Your Blame.

I love you My Brother/Sister and you will Get Through. Because God has Provided, and I'm Praying for You.

From Not Qualified To Chosen

I don't have the Greatest Resume. But I have a Testimony. Believe me I've Traveled Far, listen as I Share My Journey. On paper I am Qualified to Live Among the Multitude. But My Spirit Says I Live in a Royal Altitude. My Tongue Speaks of My Limited Education. My Soul Speaks of a Higher Destination. I didn't get here by believing in doubt and the impossible. My Faith and Strength Told Me That Anything is Possible.

You see, I threw away fear, I kept doubt Frozen. Because I went From not Qualified to Chosen. I wasn't looking for an Opportunity, I was just being me. Praising God, while I was Keeping My Mind Free. I didn't hate on other's blessings, because it was not mine. Look up to God and He said "Trust Me, You'll Be Elevated in Time. If you Read My Word, You'll Find the Truth. That I could Bless in anyone's mess, ask David, Esther, Moses, and Ruth. If You Look to Man, You'll Never Qualify. The Caterpillars are Cocooned Before They Become a Butterfly. In other Words, if a Caterpillar in darkness still Believes, what Makes You Think That I can't Make You Succeed? For a Position where man says you don't Belong. But My Wisdom Says That They Are Wrong. Trust in Me, Their Requirements Will Be Frozen. Because I Made You From Not Qualified to Chosen."

Hallelujah!!!!! It's Not Me, To God Be the Glory. Trust Him, Because He's Writing Your Story. You all will Always be a part of Me. Because Our Stories are Written in History. And While the Swift and Strong looks Good Posing. You'll Be Sitting in Royalty, Because You were Chosen.

I Love The Word Woman

Some of us have failed you, because our minds are in prison. Failure to Realize that Society, wants us to live in division. You bare our children, you're the first teachers on the planet. We at times take you for granted. I see your smile, but I also see your pain. Some of us play with your insecurities, for sexual gain. Trying to make you live inferior. Not realizing that you're the one who is Superior. We know that you're a Treasure to be found. A True Queen who knows how to hold it down.

But sometimes you forget your worth. Steadily trying to fit in a Male Dominated Earth. But we know if you know who you are, you'll Know the difference between a King, and A Fake Fallen Star. Trust in Your Process and Your Dreams. Believe that God has made you into a Queen. You are the Beauty of Words Unspoken. Remember Your Promise is the Blessing, Not Broken. I know you may not hear it, but us Kings appreciate You. Which is why our true Royalty will make a vow, and say I do. We Love You and May God send Blessings Your Way.

Know That You're Royalty

You walk with confidence, never Conceit. You speak life, death in defeat. You encourage the people you Uplift. Royalty is not only living, but it's your gift. You give Love, because you know it's the way. When it comes to respect, you don't play. But it is earned, by how you Lead. You show strength, even when you Bleed. When you encourage others, they are amazed. They can't believe who you were, back in the days. They bow to you, or they salute. You know who you are, you're an absolute. You Fight the Fight, but it's mainly against Yourself. Because you're Adding and Subtracting, Your Value and Wealth. You're Strong, but your Flesh is Weak. Your Strength is not only in Physical, it's when you speak. Your Haters are your friends, your Fans are your enemies. You Hunger for Knowledge, you're Mighty in Breed.

Remember You're a part, of a Royal Priesthood. All Things Work Together, For the Good. The Pain is Large, but so is the Lesson. You're the Promise, You're the Blessing. No Need for Validation, it's Been Declared and Decreed. God Said It's So, Trust and Believe. Wake up David, Your Goliath has been Defeated. Your Throne is yours, to be Seated. Without shame, wear your Crown, it's a part of your worth. Because You're the Greatest Inspiration, Needed on This Earth. When God Gave us Christ, he gave us his Loyalty. He's Already Called You, know that You are Royalty.

Inspired by 1 Peter 2:9, and Recognizing Your Worth.

You Are My Son

Look at you, a reflection of Me. Who will be the cure of a Generation's Disease. Because I'm not a Father who runs away without a care. Why would I, when you're the next heir. I was born without a Crown or Throne. But God Showed Me how to Build one on My Own. Which is where you come in. I can't believe that My Seed's New Life Begins. So much to do, so much to learn. I'll teach how respect is both given and earned. Because someday you'll have a seed of your own. Prayerfully you'll wait till you're fully grown. I could tell you that temptation is a lifetime fight. But you'll be equipped to put all demons to flight. Look at Me, another Victory I've Won. God made me Your Daddy, and You are My Son.

A Blessing you are, because you were created. Look at you, you're A lil Me Upgraded. Please learn from my mistakes and don't repeat them. Because you're designed to dance to a different rhythm. Women comes a dime a dozen, but a Queen comes Virtuously Free. Respect and Love her Responsibly. Because the devil also wears a blue dress. Consult to God as to whom is your life's invest. If she's your inspiration, make her your Priority. Lead her to God, and lift her esteem with Authority. Because You're Her and Our Family Representation. Show her that her Love is one of your destinations.

Now that you're here I'm going to do My Best. To keep it real to you no matter the test. Because that's what a Father does for his seed. You're More Inspiring than any master's degree. You're a Prince who'll grow in to a King. A leader, a Master of your craft, You're Life's Meaning. Growing into a Man can be overwhelming. Because your life is a message developing. Don't take for granted as to whose you are. Because the World looks up to your rising star.

106

Dwayne J. Torres

You're Destined for greatness; a new legacy has Begun. You're My Blessed Child, You are My Son.

The Encounter

I'm His Child, Adopted By The Blood

Me: I'm Grateful Father God, for Your Son Jesus, and The Holy Spirit. My Life was Spent, but you've Delivered it. I am not worthy of the adoption, but Jesus Paid the Cost. Thank You for Re-Directing Me, when I Was Lost. I thought I was The Greatest Sinner, but You Still Chose Me. How can one with a Lost Vision, Still be able to See? It's Because You Said "Yes, Come sit at My Table. That even in Troubled Times, I'll show you That I am Able. To Love You Past Your Flaws, now what were They? I already Forgot, Because I was Listening to You Pray." That's why I Love You Lord, because Nothing Could Ever Separate us. Still have My back, even when I'm not in focus. Thank You for Raising the Standards, when the enemy comes like a Flood. Thank You for Adopting, Me Under the Blood.

God: Why would I not Adopt You? Welcome to My Family. But You were always a member, Jesus's Blood Bought in the Harmony. Your sins made you Believe, that you're not worthy. But it was your spirit, who stayed hungry and thirsty. It hungered for a word, and it thirsted for peace. Which is why I've diminished your poverty, and sent in Your Increase. I know at times you felt like I wasn't there. Life gotten so rattled you thought that I didn't care. But I work best when I'm Silent and Whisper. Which is why your spirit was never shaken or shivered. I Love You Too Much for You to Lose Your Way. Which is why I'm very attentive when you Pray. Nothing Could Ever Separate Me from You, My Child. Lift up your Head, Believe, Decree, and Smile. Like the Ark, I'll Protect You from The Flood. You're Declared My Child, By The Blood.

Why I've Doubted You

Our Flesh: I've tried to believe in you, but My Fear Doubted. It's no excuse for this, but my fears spoke the loudest. I don't deserve your help, nor your Love. Because I didn't want to believe that you're from God above. Yes, you've performed miracles, yet I don't see a difference. But it was amazing to see, how demons flee from your mere Presence. Pharisees says that you can't be real, because there's still a lot of evil. They say Adam was the Son of Man, and you're the Sequel. In other words, you're just like him you're a sinner. Sorry to speak blasphemy but when it comes to that, they say you're the winner. I see the world I'm in, and it's hard to cope. When I call on you, it seems like there's no hope. I don't get the answer that I'm looking for. Every time I look up there's another closed door. Forgive me Lord, but there's nothing else to do. I'm on a sinking ship called life, which is why I doubted You.

Jesus: My Brother/Sister why is it that you do not see? I've Chosen you to follow me. You got so caught up in your environment, it's your Blessings you don't see. Oh, ye of little faith, why do you really doubt? Especially when you were drowning, I've pulled you out. Your doubt is stopping you from Excellency. I rose again on the third day, so you could live in an Expectancy. So if My Father could deliver me, Son of Man, what makes you think you won't reach your Promise Land? You allow yourself to live in fear. But you always overcome year after year. The Doors that were closed was for your protection. The Doors that are open are a part of your Elevation. So put away your fear, erase your doubts and follow me. Because I'm the one who'll keep you in perfect peace. I call you to walk in Faith, Be with Her. You are My Brother/Sister a Believer.

I'm Not Excusing, But I'm Human

Me: I see the nails, I've placed them there. My sins are flowing without a care. My doubts and fears lurked about. My Transgressions speak with a loud shout. My volume turned up, My Morality is Down. My Sins treated you, like you were a Circus Clown. You speak peace, but I went deaf. You've delivered My Soul, but I am a total mess. You've directed my path, but I got lost. I never thought your life would be the cost. I've laughed at you, and beat you senseless. I even denied you before a witness. I'm so sorry, that I'm a part of your story. Of how you were mistreated before you went to glory. I should've loved you more as God Commands. I'm not Excusing myself, but I am Human.

Jesus: My Precious Brother of Mine, why do you weep? When I told you before that I'm your Forever Keep? I have Forgiven You while nailed on the Cross. Your debt was paid in full, My Blood paid The Cost. Faint Not, my arms come with Grace and Mercy. I died for you because of Love, and Not as a Courtesy. The Prophesy was fulfilled and Now I'm with our Father. He's still preparing a table for you, he desires you to prosper. You allowed your sins to hold you guilty to your case. But I'm your Courtroom Lawyer, look at My Face. I didn't condemn You or your sins. I'll see you in paradise, the devil never wins. You're covered with Flesh with emotions, that makes you Human. Your Promise will be fulfilled, as I intercede for the Son of Man. God Loves You and So do I. Keep your Faith and Love Like Heaven's Eyes.

We Are Here To Worship

We Don't mean no harm, we just wanted to Pray. We just wanted to worship God, No Matter What Time of Day. Excuse Me? But what did we do so wrong? Is it because we've prayed a lil bit too Long? I could understand that we could be Long Winded. But how can you Not Thank God, For All of The Sins He's Amended? You see, we were on our way to hell. God Prevented us from Giving Nebachnezar our Souls to Sell. So he used us to show him that we're the exception to the Rule. That No Weapon can pierce God's children while he Holds our Mule.

God Loves Nebachnezar, that he wanted him to see and Be Amazed. That God can cover his Children while Giving Him Praise. Which is what we were doing, Inside of the fiery furnace hot and sweltering. While God had his Ministering Angels with us while he was Sheltering.

We've never forgotten about our lessons learned. Just because the devil sends fire, doesn't mean you'll get burned. You see even when the devil sends the Heat, your Anointing sends it in retreat. The devil never wins, and that he knows. Because he can't stop the Blood or Favor from overflow. So please excuse us, but we have a God to Praise. Blessed is what it feels like to have your Soul Raised. If you're ever in a bind, Tell the devil your Soul is not for purchase. Just Go to God in Prayer and Worship.

I Want To See Me Through Your Eyes

I forget My Purpose, and I Lose My Faith. I struggle with My Spirit, Sometimes it's a Debate. I see how you blessed others, but what about me? Maybe if you remove the spiritual cataracts, then I can see. Excuse Me Father for my rude and blunt Nature. It's just when it comes to me, I don't see the Favor. Distractions are Heavy and I Lose My Focus. I am suffering from despondency, a Spiritual Locust. You created My Life, and I want to live it. I want to partake on what's happening and what you exhibit. I guess the only way, is to see me through your eyes. Then Maybe I can see My Cause and My Prize?

God: Oh My Precious Child, why do we always have the same conversations? But I am pleased that you want to see you from My Observations. I've seen the sins you've committed, but that's not you. Allow Me to continue to Encourage, Like I do. I've observed your past, but that's not you either. Because I could use anyone, a drunk, an adulterer, and a fouled mouth Peter. You've made mistakes, but you're a Human Being. It's not your faults that I concentrate on seeing. It's your Soul that I look into. Hoping you'll see My Holy Spirit inside of You. If it's favor you seek, I supply it daily. The air you breathe, the sunlight and the waters waving. You've mentioned spiritual cataracts so that you can see? That speck of judgment that you've implemented towards your brothers, sisters, and Me? But Don't worry, nothing is held anything against you. Because Grace and Mercy, is daily Provided too. It's Like Favor Given in advance.

Utilize your Faith, and take that chance. I've already supplied all of your needs. I always hear you when you speak from your knees. So when I see you, I see Fearfully and Wonderfully Made. My Lil Kings and Queens, My Forever Love Expose'.

Inspired by Matthew 7:3

God: Trust Me I Got You

God: I've realized you went astray. It's ok, because I still love you. Some won't recommend, believing I'll condemn, But it's not true. I created you to succeed and live life abundantly. No condemnation so you can confess, I won't Love You any less. If any I'll Love You More, because you trusted, and I adore. You've utilized Love and Faith, I give you Mercy and Grace.

So don't believe the hype, when they say you're not my type. But How Can You be, when I created you for me? I understand some misgivings; false prophets are so misleading. Telling fables and fairytales, saying its heaven when it's hell. But I'm here for you to tell, send back that devil's mail.

You have fallen for his lies, and fell down and wondered why? I allowed it so you can see, how to get back up and be free. You may not realize but it's you I've considered. To show the devil that you're a true winner. Mistakes will happen, and you're not perfect. The storms will pass, the lessons are worth it. If you come to me bold but humble, I'll anoint your path, while your haters mumble. They probably think I'm just playing, no never, Just Love displaying. To those who want to know the truth. Designed your purpose before your youth. I give seeds of blessings, while forever professing.

You're My Child, My seed. Although we don't always agree. But My son Jesus will intercede. He died for you, so release your stress. He takes in all heavy laden and missteps. Always asking for your forgiveness.

Don't worry about the devil, his demons and what men do. Be still and Know That I am God, Trust Me I Got You.

Set Me Free Lord

Me: I'm in prison, of my mind that's filled with depression and doubt. I want to know more of what my life is all about. Your word speaks of freedom, if I truly believe. But so many false prophets walking, it's hard not to feel deceived. You marvel when I speak of faith, your word says it pleases you. But with so many versions of your story, it's hard to decipher which is true. My mind is so cluttered with mess and stress. I have people tell me don't worry it's just a test. Really? They can't feel my pain of what I go through. Like rising above it all is easy to do. Yeah but it's ok to judge my sins, point the finger and say that I'm to blame. Walk around with my head down and feel so ashamed. I know following you won't be easy, never said it would be. But God I need you because I need to be free.

God: I want you to look into a mirror and look at its reflection. Each waking Day I send My Angels to cover for your protection. You talk of pain yeah, but I sent it on purpose. How Can You be a soldier if you're not Nerveless? You can't fight into your controlled battles with fear. You are an Overcomer, so speak life into the Atmosphere. You have a powerful weapon and it's called your tongue. You are the David to your Goliath, so you've already won. Stop under estimating your talents, because of a few that hates. I can give it to someone else who wouldn't hesitate. To become all I desire for them to be. Take a good look at yourself, you are free. Don't look to others for they don't know my plan. They'll try their best, but never understand. Don't fear the storms because it's a blessing. It'll give you growth, so embrace your lesson. A lesson that overcome challenges and give you favor. Who could stand the tests of time, while uplifting your neighbor. Now you can correct, and not be judgmental. You can assist me by spreading my love and they'll be grateful. Don't ever take for granted of what you mean to me. Open up your heart, live and see that you are Free.

Faithful

Dwayne J. Torres

Lord, I'm Ready

Father I'm bowing down Like I'm supposed to do. Please Allow me to reintroduce Myself to You. I am Your Child, who wants to reach your shores. I no longer want to sail on waters of trouble and Lures. I want to be the head, upon your instructions. I can't take anymore of Life's deductions. But it had to go away, because I must conform. To your ways Lord, so I can be Transformed. Like a Butterfly, breaking away from its cocoon. I want to be Changed, Forever in tune. Learning from My Mistakes, by taking ownership. Confessing My Sins, on my way to discipleship. You see Lord, I love the way how you Choose. An Evader, A Murderer, and A Farmer who Drank Booze. But that's no excuse for me to sin. I just want to have a relationship with you again.

I've stayed away, because I was ashamed. I was too busy looking into the world for some fame. Whenever I had faults, I've pointed to others to blame. But the reality is no one knew My Name. But this why I want to come back home to you. Because My Spirit feels Caged, like a Lion in a Zoo. I know now that you are in full control. Because you are My Keeper of Life, and My Soul. Your Love for Me is so incredible. Which is why to you Lord I'm Available. No more will I be imbalanced, I'm standing Steadily. Here I am Lord, I'm Ready.

Lord, I'm Available To You

Father, Please Hear the words that I Pray. I'm turning My Life over to you, I give Myself Away. You've tried to Reach me, but I went Prodigal. Insecurities and Doubt Made You Impossible. I didn't believe that I was Your Responsibility. Because of Sin I didn't think I was your Priority. So I continued My Life thinking I had no meaning. No purpose, No Positivity, No Reason Being. I was so withdrawn, that depression and I became Friends. Would I ever fall in Love? Hmm, that all depends. If they weren't on my level, they weren't worthy. But how can I judge them, when I'm the one living thirsty? Oh Father I really want to know your Glory. But too many Preachers sell rather than tell your Story. How can I repent when you are being sold? You won't bless me unless I pay, I'm being told. Some of the congregation have their noses up in the air. Making Me Believe that you really don't care.

Sometimes when I read your word, I feel so illiterate. With the guilt of sin, A Defeated Mind is deliberate. But That's why I don't feel close to you. Because of the sins that I've done and will do. (Crying) But Jesus..... But Jesus... Jesus told me that it's I whom you Believed in. That I don't have to live in fear or be defeated. I have so much in life, that I need to live for. But I'm way too focused at the wrong doors. I've never noticed the ones that you have opened for me. Because of My Transgressions, My Faith went Empty. According to you Lord, My Sins are Forgiven. That's why I want, to change the way that I'm Livin'.

You've promoted Me, despite My Misbehaving. Thank You Lord For taking in My Heavy Laden's. Today I'm surrendering My Life and all of things that I do. Now and Forevermore Lord, I am Available to You. In Jesus Name I Pray Amen

Inspired by Matthew 11:28-29, The Gospel Song "Lord, I'm Available To You" And To All Those Who Struggle Between Society and Spirit.

A Child's Prayer

Dear God, I'm praying unto you. My Mommy and Daddy is in the other room praying too. But they don't know about my prayer. Because they don't know how much you Love and care. They say that they do. But to me they don't have a clue. Maybe it's because it's been a while since they left home. Sometimes I feel like I'm on My Own. I see them worry about bills and other adult stuff. But I don't understand all of the fuss. Because you take care of the Birds and they still fly. Don't know when their next meal is, but you still supply. Maybe it's the television that has their mind twisted? Or that thing they call social media, Please Jesus fix this. I hear Daddy say he Lost his Job, My Mommy comforts him. I heard him say that we may have to move again. But that's ok because you'll be there. Maybe I can tell My Friends about you, I Like to Share.

Wait, they're singing, they must of finished praying. Maybe they do have a clue as to whom they're Praising. Wow, I just heard Dad saying The Devil is a Liar. My Mom yelled that we're lifting Jesus Higher. Oh, I get it now Lord, they are having Faith. That Pleases You God, wow that is so Great. Because Now I truly know for sure, that you're going to bless us with so much more. Now I can't sit still because I'm so Happy. Thank You Lord for My Mommy and Daddy. I see their fight and together we'll stand. Yes, My Parents Do Understand. To keep Trusting and Believing. Through Jesus we will always be exceeding. One Last thing God, before I Go. I just want to let the devil know.

God stopped your traps and your snares. Because you're No Match to a Child's Prayer. Thank You God it's another Win. In Jesus Name I Pray, Amen, Amen, and Amen.

Inspirationally Redeemed

My Overcomer, My Achiever

Me: Father God, I've read what you've done for Job. And I Know That You can do it For Me. You made me aware of your power. You've made a Blind Man see. But why do I still feel that it's not enough? Every step I take gets harder and rough. Is it that I'm looking at the wrong message? Or I'm too focused on the presage? My Soul cries for you, My Tears Flow like Rivers and Fountains. But a Mustard Seed was Planted, and I was able to Move Mountains. I've stretched My Hand out to you, because I was Hanging from a Cliff. Then you gave me wings to soar, My Soul has Lift. My Flesh was leading me to My Lust, Temptation Almost Destroyed My Existence. But then your Anointing Destroyed the Yoke, Because Jesus was very Persistent. On Making Sure He Paid My Debt with his Blood. Powerfully He did it for me, Raising the Standard against the devil's flood. I want to thank you Lord, because I've come to Realize, that every Trial and test is just a Blessing in Disguise. I apologize for not realizing this earlier in My Walk. No Longer feeling like My Spirit is being Stalked. Thank You Father for Your Grace, Mercy, and Love. I Thank You for Being God, From Heaven Above.

God: My Precious Child, I'm excited that you've learned your Lessons. I'll make sure your cup overflows with My Love and Blessings. You see it's not every day that you speak of Faith. Especially When Satan attacks, uses your Flesh as Bait. To capture the Vile Spirits to plant in your Soul. But it can never pierce through a Heart made of Platinum raised From Gold. You are Mightier than Sampson, Humble Like Moses. Patient Like Joseph, your Soul never opposes.

To all that I have for you. Completing My Plan is what you'll do. I Love You My Child Because through it all, you Never Stopped Being a Believer. Which is why I Declare You, My Overcomer, My Achiever.

Inspired by Job 38 – 41

I Had A Meeting With God

I was late, but God was on time. He still Blessed Me, because it was about him, not about my grind. He let me know that I was on a mission. At first, I misunderstood his decision. Why would he choose me, a broken vessel? God said that's the best way to confuse The Devil.

God: I know that you have suffered long. But your faith is rebuilding, and your purpose is strong. So I chose you because you wouldn't volunteer. Not realizing that there's strength in your tears. I heard your cries and your silent prayers. Which is why you're chosen because your spirit Loves and your Soul cares. You speak to others even when you're broken. Which is why you're favored and chosen. Don't worry I'll be with you if anyone opposes. Give you strength in your words, like I did for Paul and Moses. I understand that you weren't always on the straight and narrow. But what I'll give you will defeat demons and the armies of Pharaoh. So, my son, I'm giving you this mission because I know you can. I want you to demonstrate the trials, yet Favor of a Kingdom Man. So do you accept this mission and Do your Best?

My answer to you Lord God, is Yes. Sorry I was late, but thank you God for all that you do.

God: It's My Pleasure Son, and I Love You.

Dwayne J. Torres

When God Says No

I thought he punished me, but it was for my protection. He was perfecting my spirit, so we can have a real connection. I took a look at Myself and thought I had no purpose. That was nothing but the devil, because he got nervous. Because he knew if I realized as to who I am, that God gives me wisdom to destroy the devil's plan. When God Says No, it's not a setback it's a blessing. Because Father Knows Best is a real life's lesson. His goal is for us to stay focused and stand tall. Trust and believe you won't have far to fall. God's No is like a Grandmother's Yes. Happily received Glorious Success. You know that feeling when grandma says yes. You can eat some ice cream but clean up your mess. Your Greatest Blessing comes when God Says No. Because your Greatest Testimony will be Told. It'll give his people joy and hope. Because of God's Audacity of Nope. So thank God for he's our absolver. Our Father Our Lord, our Problem Solver. Thank you Father God you knew better, protecting us from fear, our stormy weather. You did it for us because you love us so. Our Spirits are in perfect peace because of your no. Thank You.

The Wait

It's our greatest gift, our greatest Tradition. Some see it as a Blessing, some as affliction. We cannot stop it once it's in transition. But don't worry, there's a purpose for its mission. It strengthens while you are weak. You think negatively once it reaches peak. Doubt starts to appear, then it invites discouragement and fear. But You must understand its language, its culture. It teaches like the Angel at the Sepulcher. Reiterates its mission the language translates. Into a metaphorically spirit that resonates. Then you later understand, that it was all a part of God's Plan. So he can get the Glory, by telling your testimony. How you overcame the storm. Gaining strength and Faith beyond the norm. It's always on time, it's never late. Learning that you're blessed, during the wait. It teaches patience, it creates envy. It gives joy to your enemies. Because they believe you're stuck at a setback. But it's really a warm up to your comeback. That's what makes this so Great. The coming out after the anticipate. Have Blessings flowing like rivers. It's enthusiasm always delivers. A new driven life has begun. Because you believed in Isaiah 40:31. Even though there's a lot at stake. Remember that there's a Blessing in The Wait.

Inspired by Isaiah 40:31

Dwayne J. Torres

The Backup Praise

A strong storm can make a Hospital lose its power. That's when a Generator is used to backup for hours. When things get rough, and you're about to quit, don't get discouraged, because God Already has you Equipped. On how you're going to get through this hallucinational maze. He indwelled reinforcements to back up your praise.

He placed it in you upon your conception. Because he knew that one day, you'll lose your connection. Like a cell phone signal with only one bar. He won't allow you to get but so far. So He gives you an angelic Wi-Fi and your praise is your PIN. Placed within your soul, and that's where your faith begins. Distractions come fierce like a Dog in Heat. But you're more superior with Control, Alt, and Delete. The devil's goal is to kill, steal, and destroy, to get you downhearted. But the Heavenly Angels have already been imparted. It's in you since your day of birth. Reminds you (when you allow) to know your worth.

When demons come in like a disease, your back up praise puts them at ease. There's not a praise that God won't permit, which means the devil has to submit. The Angels over you are preparing your fight. Your praises send over 1,000 demons to flight. You're provided with a Royalty of Dominance and Flair. Decreasing the evil pneuma that's sucking up your Blessed air.

So remember, to have a relationship with The Creator. So you'll know how to utilize your Praise Generator.

Don't Allow your sin to prevent you from God's Relations. Because he's setting you up to be a Blessing to All Nations. Don't be afraid, you'll get through this part of life's phase. Surrender to God, and don't neglect your praise.

You've Kept Me!

Whenever I think of you through the years of Joy and Pain, I Never thought of giving up, but there was so much Rain. There were times when I felt I was moving in reverse. I had no idea of how many Angels that was disbursed. To protect me and mine so we could live, in peace and harmony with so much Love to give. Many try to convince me that you were a lie. Like there's no after world when I die. Some say you aren't there, some say that I'm forgotten. But you gave us Jesus your son the only Begotten. I am Forever Grateful that you never stopped being who you are and believing. That's why I pray with Love and Thanksgiving. Thank You for allowing Life and your splendor of Earth and waters deep. Thank You God, for all of the years that You've Kept Me.

Inspirationally Redeemed

God Is Calling Your Name

Lord, I hear you calling me, but what am I to do? I'm not the kindest person, I'm not the one for you to choose.

I've cursed at you, I've said your name in vain. I used people for both money and sexual gain.

Remember last year, I've murdered a Man. I fornicate at every cost, all of the sex I could stand.

I'm angry because my Parents weren't there. I got into a relationship with someone who doesn't really care.

You called for me to be a leader, all I know how to do is follow. It seems like I'm the weakest link, while the devil is strong like Apollo.

Why do you have me living in Poverty? I don't even have a story to my Biography.

I am just a vessel without water in my veins. My sins have a large amount of crimson stains.

But you still chose me, which I don't understand. I'm not even worthy to be called a man.

My woman left me, and I don't spend time with my Kids. They still hate me, for all of the wrong things that I did.

I don't deserve your love or your mercy. But I do thank you for giving me Jesus as a common courtesy.

I don't take ownership, I point fingers to give blame. But yet I still hear your Angels Calling My Name.

God: My Child, Yes, My Angels and I are calling you out. Because what you have done in this life, is not what you're all about.

I know who you are, I know where you've been. Don't forget my Son's blood already paid for your sins.

You have to understand that I Love You. I call you by your name, not what your sins do.

You are one of my reasons why I've created life. Don't Worry about that woman who left, she was not your wife.

Your Children Love you, and they want their Dad. They want to experience the love from their Father, something you wish you had.

But I stood in place for him, and I've watched you for years. I was there when you were crying your silent tears.

So yes, I'm calling you because you are my Child. I'll continue to protect you, like the Animals in the Wild.

You were born to be in a place of Greatness. Success will only place you in a city of fools, and a whole lot of fakeness.

You Don't Live in Poverty, That's Just the State of Mind. The truth is you drank the blood of beer, and not the divine wine.

Don't allow your past or your sin Cripple your calling. I'll catch you and give you wings from falling.

So Live and enjoy, you can go on and state your claim. For I am God, and I'm Still Calling Your Name.

Deliverance

Dwayne J. Torres

I've Been Redeemed

I've played with Hearts, I Lived My Fame. I belittle your goals, with no shame. I was superficial, I was selfish and Mean. I was living the life, that many of you envy. I tell you stories that's already been told. I almost agreed with Satan to sell My Soul. I didn't know My Purpose, so I've followed a Path. But I've should've known, that it wasn't going to last. There was no future, because the path wasn't mine. Love had no meaning, because it was hard to Find. I knew a lot, but not My Purpose. I Played My Life, like a 3 Ring Circus. Don't ask about My sins, it's in the past. I do need a change and I need it fast. What can I Say, or what can I Do? Where can I escape, who can I Run Too?

So then I've decided to go to Church. I heard of Jesus and did some research. About a man who died upon the Cross. Who saved My soul, when I was Lost. I wanted to know more about this man. Not realizing it was a part of God's Plan. He had wanted me, to come into repentance. And Give Up the habit, of Co-dependence. Trust that I was willing, to take a chance. Depression and Oppression took its Last Dance. I also Found out that I was never alone. Jesus Prayed for Me, to God on The Throne. Jesus was always, on My Side. Take me to the Water Lord, I want to be Baptized.

I want to thank you Lord, for letting me see. Of how you wanted My Soul to be set free. Rescuing My Spirit from a devil's Hell. I could only imagine, of the Testimony that I will tell. On how you saved My Soul, From a demonic regime. Then You Declared, that I've Been Redeemed.

If I Could Just Touch

I saw you coming, but I didn't think I was worthy. I'm too much of a mess, I'm too Worldly. But I've heard a Rumor that you could heal. But My issues have told me to be still. Because what would a man like you, want with me? I feel like you'll be like others and watch me bleed. But there's something about you that's different from man. You sound as if you're a part of a bigger plan. People parade around you, like you're a celebrity. But they also ridicule you, so incredibly. But as I said there's something about you, I don't know what it is. You have this aura about you, that you even receive love from kids.

All My Life I didn't walk quickly; Heck I don't walk at all. Because My issue slows me down, all I do is Crawl. I see that you're on your way, to a girl who's probably dead. Just one touch from you, she'll be alive and Fed. Yes, that one touch and I'll be made Whole. With 2 Fish and 5 Loaves of bread, you Fed 5,000 Souls. If I could just get a little closer, it'll be so appealing. Just A Touch of Your Garment, I can Start My Healing. You're Not too far, but I better move fast. So I could rid of these issues at last.

Oh My God, he's heading this way. Maybe if I call him, what would I say? Will he take a moment to help little ole me? What is there to lose, or just let it be? He's arriving now but how can I reach him? The light from the sky is getting real dim. But what if he finds out about My sins? How can I justify, where would I begin? It doesn't matter now, because I'm bleeding too much. I'm getting weaker, all I need is just one touch. Relieve Me from this issue, My Soul's been Tainted. Just one touch, please Oh God! My Body has fainted.....

Jesus: Wake up My Dear Sweet Sister, it's not time for you to go. Your Faith has brought you to me, you've been made whole. Look at you, your issues are gone. Get up and walk, your bones are now strong. Those who over looked you, will now believe. That even in brokenness you can still Achieve. With me, you can do all things. Look at all of the joy, that you'll bring. Go your way and live in peace. And tell everyone, that you personally know Me.

Inspired by Mark 5.

Return To Sender

Dear Male Sinner, how are You? Thought you had a friend, where's your crew? Oh yeah, you pray to God who sent them away. But I remember how you were back in the days. You were a pimp player, a Mack if you will. Having women at your lair for sexual thrills. Did you ever once make any of them your Queen? You've dismissed them, and crumble their beautiful self-esteem? I also saw how you said that you'll shelter them through rain and blizzards. You're More Phony than the man who pretended to be The Wizard. You tell them that you're a great outstanding King. Sounding like lyrics from a song that a fool would sing. You never finished what you started. Your kids look for you and become down hearted. Now you talk about praying by getting on your knees? I remember when you worshipped 40's and weed. You're a poor excuse of man, even a muted human can tell. Signed Sealed and Delivered, the Letter from Hell.

Dear Female Sinner, how are You? Don't catch no attitude with me because, a man never stayed true. It's your fault because he told you the truth. I guess you should've been more patient, like Esther and Ruth. What did you expect, from a guy with no respect? He was there for sex, not for your heart and soul to protect. Look at You, a failure of a Woman living unhappily. How can you talk about others, when you're not living phenomenally? Now Praying to 'Some God' on your knees? How can you pray, when your Children are in need? You're such a sad sight even a blind man can tell. Signed Sealed and Delivered, the Letter from Hell.

God: My Precious Child, let me make something perfectly clear. This is a letter that you don't have to adhere. But no matter what the devil says, whether true or fake, My Son Jesus sacrificed his life, for Love and your Sake. Satan may have pointed out, some of your past sins. But it was washed away with The Blood of Jesus, your Soul is Forgiven. Your sins maybe a part of your story. But let it go, it has no authority. Over you or your destination. I've chosen you without hesitation. The Envelope was sealed with a brimstone smell. Stamp Return to Sender, and I'll send The Letter Back to The Pits of Hell.

Operating on the Wrong Esteem

God: I see your passion, but you think it's a facade. You think it's unattainable, you think it's odd. How can you proclaim your someday, when you don't pursue success My way? Ok, I understand how it may look. But work with me and Read My Book. I've already instructed you on how to succeed. Although you think My stories are hard to believe. Like How can I have a man part The Red Sea? Because he was not operating on the Wrong Esteem. Before you start, Look at Your Past. As You can see, I won't allow trouble to last. In my book there's another story. About a man who lived on his Father's Glory. He took his inheritance and played the field. Later found himself without a Dollar Bill. He realized pursuing the superficial had him eating crumbs like a mouse. He became wise, and went back to his Father's House. Lesson learned, don't pursue the dollar, pursue the dream. You will fail operating on the Wrong Esteem.

Here's another Story from My Book. About a Woman who had the Look. Of a Beautiful Rose people would say. But many men had her their way. Yet they wanted to stone her and place her in hell. Each of them had a story to tell. So My son Jesus told them to go ahead. Stone her, but only the ones without sins instead. Neither could cast, because they had seen. That they were all operating on the Wrong Esteem. So listen carefully, to My Whispers and follow My Instructions. If you follow another's path, you'll fall into self-destruction. I've created you to be a Superstar. Given you wings of an Eagle, so you can Soar Far. I've declared you a Lifetime Commitment. You are no longer Spiritually Impotent. You are My Greatest Creation made of My Image. Winning the game of life is only a Scrimmage. I will fulfill your visions, declared it done and Decreed. Continue to Trust and Believe in Me. There's nothing you won't be able to achieve. By operating your Faith and the Right Esteem.

The Calm After The Storm

It rained, it poured, winds blew. But still God said I Got You. The eye hovered, the clouds darkened. Escaping to his shelter, My Soul was Pardoned. Because the Storm had come like it Should. It worked out basically for My Good. Without any Storms, I couldn't Grow. Strengthening My Faith, I've come to Know. The Storm was all a part of God's Will. When it had gotten rough, Jesus declared Peace Be Still. Satisfying my prayers, I knew a storm would come. To blow away any unnecessary fetishism and demonic crumbs. While I'm rebuilding from damages abroad, God renovated My Soul, oh Thank You Lord. Standing on his word, I knew that it wouldn't last. Why not? God always came through for me in the Past. It may have caused people to leave, and relationships severed. But that's nothing new you haven't heard. Because not everyone is a part of the equation. They were a part of My Journey, not My Destination. Yes, it hurt to let them go. I don't know why, but they would've cut My Flow. But that doesn't make them a bad person. It's just God said they had fulfilled their purpose. They were there for a life learned lesson. Come to think about it, they were a part of My Blessing. So remember my Brothers and Sisters, Trouble don't last Always. Which is why we should expect your miracle any day. As you can see that there are no weapons that are Formed Against you, because there's always calm before and after the Storm.

That Look of Peace Within

Swallowed Pride, Threw Away pain. Rejected Fleshy thoughts, only Solace Remained. My Trial was over, My Verdict was Clear. Not Guilty was the call, after suffering for years. Your Prisoned mind could be a Lifetime Sentence. But with Jesus as your Lawyer, it's an automatic Acquittance. Because a debt was paid long ago, your blessings about to overflow. Jesus went to the Cross at Calvary. Which means that you're not the devil's statistic or category. Your past doesn't dictate your directive obligation. That's the devil's way of leading your future into the wrong Destination. So remember that you're the Apple of God's Eye. Captures your tears Every time you've cried. Don't worry, God already promised that you'll win. Jesus already asked God to forgive your sins. We all know that God, Jesus, and The Holy Spirit are One. Before you even stepped into the Ring, you've already won. No need to look any further. Body, Mind, and Soul already had been Nurtured. So sleep tonight with this in mind. That the peace you're looking for, is not hard to find. Situations May have you believing that you're Blind. But God made a Blind Man see, and calls you a Child of Mine. So let Go and Rejoice. Because God heard your Soul's Voice. Sunshine is there, even when it rains. Look at all of the Favor that You'll gain. Starting Line is here, your new life Begins. Now go to your mirror, Look at Purpose and your Peace Within.

The Starting Line is Waiting

God's word says Faith without works is dead. Which is why we need to escape the comfort zone and be Led. No journey comes without trials and tribulations. Resisting the devil's lies and try avoiding temptation. It's easy to fall prey to all of the devil's works and traps. Especially When he plays with your mind, stating your journey has no maps. But you must remember that the devil is a liar. Because he knows once you get started, you'll be lifting Jesus Name even Higher. You don't have a map, but your spirit knows where you are going. God already set your eternal navigation system, the devil hopes that you'll be ignoring. Flesh then tells you that you're lost. Whatever happened to you, I thought you were the boss.

Making you feel inadequate just to say the least. But you are equipped to kill the beast. Because you are not a Slave to your flesh. Put on the armor of God, and wear his bullet proof vest. You are meant for Greatness, planted in you since birth. Which is why you feel hindrances towards your worth. But you are going to soar. Rising above all, because inside of you there's so much more. Your Destiny awaits you, it's called: There. But first you must leave your place called: Compare. God did not give you an address with man's name on the mortgage. Stop hoarding past mistakes in your subconscious storage. Because where you're going, you have to leave that behind. Truth, Love, answers, and Legacy is what you'll find. Not at the end of the Rainbow, but at the end of the valley. You'll arrive at Success, but that's not the only Grand Finale.

Your final destination is Glory, People will be telling and selling your story. So get up and stop your hesitating. The Starting Line is Waiting.

Inspired by: Hebrews 10:36 Colossians 1:11 1 Corinthians 10:13 James 1:2-3

Inspirationally Redeemed

I'm Not Dead, I Am Free

My Life was going in a different direction, a Life I came to know. It's not for the faint of heart, I've lost my inner glow. I allowed men to judge me, and base it as My worth. It seems like they only respect those with low esteem, and who twerk. Depression becomes me, and My children are looking at me funny. Men approaching me are either with no vision, or unexplained money. Then they say that they're kings, ignore their hats with bells. (Jesters) Sexing me saying yeah, I make you feel good, but I feel like I'm in hell. I thought to myself as I Lay alone in my bed, there has to be a better way, well at least I'm not dead.

Then it hit me, Yes, I'm not Dead I am free. Yes, my experiences made me feel as if I've died. But according to God's word that devil kills, steals, and destroys, yes, he's a lie. So why did I listen to a snake, when God said I'll soar? I was created to birth a nation, I'm worth so much more. I'm the first teacher, The World comes to know. I was born to be a Queen, not some fool's ho. Jesters approach me and say they'll be the best I'll ever have in life. While trying to play me for a guppy, and never making me their wife. Leave me alone jester, and make way for my King. The one who leads me to Christ, while I spread my wings. I'll celebrate My newfound Life, by taking me up in flight. Destroying all depressions, insecurities with my Dignity and fight. My flesh made up this lie, but my depression was nothing but phantom. A Woman who is wonderfully and Phenomenally made, should have her own National Anthem.

Blowing from the dust, I'm Moving Forward while Believing, Loving the God in Me. Because Glory Be to God, I'm not Dead, I am Free.

Inspired by Mark 5:35-42

Let It Go...You Don't Live There

Flesh: Tired and weary, is one way of describing My Pain. Couldn't believe that what I have inside of me has sustained. I want to live in peace, but do I really want that experience? Especially when the pain, although it hurts, it feels so Ebullience. Yes, I know it sounds absurd, but can you blame me? I know, but how can I trust a God who I cannot see? Blasphemy you scream, but look at my scars. Why is it when I call on him, he seems so far? This is not how I'm supposed to live. Almost every wealthy preacher is asking me to give. I can't give what I don't have, especially when I'm on My Last. Don't get me started on Relationships. I gave it my all, and still get the pink slip. So don't you dare tell me, that everything is going to be alright. Look at My bruises and marks from my daily fight. I'm losing my mind, and I'm starting to digress. Oh why God? I don't feel Blessed.

God: My Child, you must understand. Every one of those events was all a part of My Plan. I Broke the Mold, when I made You. So if you take a closer look My Child, you're the breakthrough. Please stop focusing on the why. A caterpillar never questions of its turning into a Butterfly. Because it knows when cocooned, its suffering is only for a moment. It's being molded in greatness, so stop being your own opponent. I can't bless you if you're stuck at an old level. I gave you those wars, so you can defeat every new devil. Yes, he comes like wolves in a pack. I allowed it, so you can have knowledge of his attacks. I raised that standard, and it's for your benefit. I'm taking you to a place where My Favor is Limitless.

I know that you'll Love Your New Address. Which is why the priceless process. I've chosen you, because I Love You and I Care. Now Let it Go, because You and I No Longer Live There.

Inspired by Romans 8:18

I Was Created For A Reason

I'm created of his image. The Reason is beyond me. It'll take a lifetime to understand, however I'm Yearning and Breathing Free. He placed me here for a purpose, a Goal I do not know. He gave me gifts and talents, while blessings abundantly Overflows. His confidence in me is strong, like a body builder with weights. I shall trust him like the builder, I can't please God without Faith. I have to realize I'm wealthy, whether financially rich or poor. Do away with the sins I enjoy, so God can open up more doors. He didn't create me with instructions, yet his word (The Bible) are the tools. Shares the greatest lessons of My History, (Mankind) not taught in Public Schools. Science and history talk of evolution, but can't explain its being. We get so caught up in our games (Reality Tv, Social Media, Religion) we miss out on Life's True Meaning. But how can you explain what you don't understand? Why would God Love so much, that he created me a man? I guess I'll understand after I'm called back home. Till then I'll continue to live not by bread alone. Also remember that there's a Blessing in every season. Because God created you and I, Maybe Love was his Reason. When created, we became a Blessing at Birth. Which is why you know God, you Know Your Worth. Now Believe it, Receive it, Achieve it, Most of All Be it.

Dwayne J. Torres

When My Soul Surrenders

I cry out to you when I have no answers. I tried to do this on my own. Not realizing if I just trust you, I'll see that my spiritual being has grown. You never said that it'll be easy. However, you've shown me in your word. That you Bless us daily with your grace. At least that's what I've Read, Experienced and Heard. I don't know why I don't get it. Why do I still have fears and insecurities? When all I have to do is put you first. And be obedient to your Authority. You're the creator of My Life, My Spirit and Soul. Giving Glory to You God, whose Mercy I've come to Know. Lesson learned, My Spirit will definitely remember. So I Give Myself Away, here's My Life Lord, My Soul and I Surrender.

I'm Praying For You

It was not by an accident, it's definitely not a coincidence. It comes to me so naturally, I come Bold with assured confidence. In order to have a relationship, I must go to God. Seek him first humbled, with confession, no matter how hard. After an hour with him, I then declared and decreed. I don't ask for your wants, I pray for your needs. So your plans could match with his, exceeding above yours because he's God, not The Wiz. I pray for your spirit and for your soul, I pray for your mind that no demon can control. Yes, I even pray for your Body, a temple spiritual connection. I'm given the responsibility to pray for purpose protection. Too many demons have been deployed. My Prayers sends 1000's to flight, and have yokes destroyed.

You have to understand, that God made me into a Kingdom Man. To Serve as well as Love, Like Christ Loves the Church. God has given me to you, so you can end your search. While you've been praying, I'm standing here displaying. How a Kingdom Man Loves his Wife, by leading her to God and start a New Life. Yes, Temptation is going to try to influence and Blind. But if you just hold on to my hand, you'll see that God is My Guide. So I won't lead you astray, I'll lead and love you his way. Allow My Love to uplift you, and your esteem. While I declare 2 Corinthians 9:14. You Matter to me, your heart and wellbeing. Which is why I Pray to him, touching and agreeing.

Praying is not a chore, it's something that I do. So Yesterday, Today, and Forever, My Life and Soul will be Praying For You.

Inspired by 2 Corinthians 9:14

Your Promise Land

You can't move into your Promise Land with an Egypt Mentality. You were guided out of there for a reason. Now go into your Blessed Reality. It's a lifetime fulfilment, not for a season. You were held down way too long. I know that your mind needs to adjust. Those fights and battles made you strong. From the power of God, in whom we trust. Don't use your scars as a crutch. Setting up for failure and disappointment. You'll miss out on abundance as such. Unlimited blessings and your anointment appointment. I cannot stress how important it is to let go, with so much at stake. Praise God for whom all blessings flow. The Land is for yours to take. Don't just take my word. But trust you'll make it. Look how God blessed the Birds, as well as Abraham, Joseph, Moses, And David. Yes, It's a long narrative journey. But no cross, no crown, no testimony. Now go and possess what have been predestined for his glory. Being A part Of a Legacy, and lived to tell your story. Moving pass your past, victory after victory, with praying hands. Go ahead, move Forward, and dwell into your Promise Land.

Dwayne J. Torres

Love Conquers

When You're Blessed With A Queen

*Elegance, Excellence is one way to describe Royalty. But can you stand in Faith and Love her Loyally? Have you ever looked at her and said, look at My Favor? God has given me My Heart's Desire and Greater. She's not only My Story, She's the Reality to My Dream. Thank You Lord, You've Blessed Me with a Queen.
Ain't nothing Greater than to be in Love with a Beautiful Star. Especially when She Believes in The King That You Are. So I placed My Crown in Her Soul. So My Love can always have a Hold. The Crown that you see on her head is just a Symbol. The one in Her Soul doesn't Resemble. Because one is for Show and Tell. The other is for protection from hell. My Priority is to Lift her up and Her Esteem. Thank You Lord, You've Blessed Me with a Queen.*

Whether she's Gangster or Your Ride and Die. You'll walk with a pep, throw away Pride. She'll inspire your Present, Embrace your Past. Motivate your Future, wanting Your Kingdom to Forever Last. She makes you proud as She Declares You as Her King. She's your Harmony to Your Soul, the reason why your Heart Sings. She's your Favorite Girl, A Woman Supreme. You are a Champion, when You're Blessed with A Queen.

*So if you're Blessed to have a Keeper, don't Love Her Light, Love Her Deeper. Even if she starts tripping, just look into her eyes. She really wants you to grow, being a Blessing in Disguise. She's the Woman that You've Prayed For, She's the Woman of Your Dreams. Life is filled with so much Favor, when You're Blessed with A Queen.
I Thank God for her Courage and for overcoming My Nerves.*

To give God Praise and a Queen to serve. She's not only a Queen, she's My Story. She's the Reason for My Testimony. I Love her, My Thoughts to My Daydream. I am very Grateful, because I'm Blessed with a Queen.

Inspirationally Redeemed

We're In This Together

Husband: When I've found you, I wanted to Crown Your Soul. Which is why Vowing to God, was My Number One Goal. I didn't want our union without a Foundation. So I grabbed the word of God, and shared it with our next Generation. I saw something in you, that made me believe again. That I can fall completely in Love, with My Best Friend. We trusted God's word, and we stand on Solid Ground. Sinking Sand, we'll never know, because his Grace is so profound. You're My Responsibility, My Priority, My Love will never waiver. Serving You, while Serving our Lord, no vain will be in My Labor. So when I'm in my war room, I'm Praying Forever. Thanking Father God for You My Queen, I Love You, and We're in this Together.

Wife: When I first laid eyes on you, My Spirit started to sing. There was no Doubt in My Soul, that you are My King. I saw you go into your war room, and I've seen how you praise. I see how you Love me, you never cease to amaze. I Love our Foundation, I Love how we fight. Not physically with each other, but putting demons to flight. You came to me as a man on a mission. You made perfectly clear of your goals and vision. Your Faith is strong, your pride has gone, you're mightier than Apollo. So Where ever God takes you My King, trust me I'll Follow. I will serve you not as a Slave to its Master. Serve You like you serve me, the rest doesn't even matter. Because when your prayers were answered, you've Eternally Crowned My Soul. Faithfully, Respectfully, Physically, we have each other to Hold. So when I pray for you, I'm praying Forever. I Love You My King, and We're in This Together.

When I Look at You, I'm Praying For You

When I Look at the stars at night. I Think about My day. When I watch the sunrise, I'm thankful to you Lord, are the words that I say. Then I turn towards you, My Beautiful Morning After. Then I speak to God who's writing My Life's next chapter. I get ready for work, and before I go my way. I Look into your eyes, then kneel and I start to pray. Being your covering is My Main Responsibility. I am supposed to be the receptor, of God's Opportunity. The opportunity to be your Love Shelter, is My daily Goal, a promise never Broken. I accepted God's offering, My Soul attached to My Vows that was Spoken. I pray for you daily as a part of my to have and to hold. I Pray for God's Covering over your Spirit, Body, Mind, and Soul. One of the Greatest Blessings to a man is a woman. Elevating her Esteem while being her Love, Champion, and Soul Ombudsman. So when our eyes lock, my prayer is gearing towards a spiritual affection. Giving you My Crown, is for Love and your Soul Protection. My Crown is Consecrated by The Anointing of God's Rewarding. Hallowing our Union while The Angels sing and Adoring. This is what my eyes are saying, and this is what I do. It says I am Looking at My Blessed Virtuous Queen, My Love, and Baby I'm Praying for you.

A Jester's Story

I'm really a King, I mean I speak his language. I'm no bellhop, but I carry a lot of baggage. I tell jokes and demand a lot of attention. I can make you feel good for a moment, but that's your decision. I can make you feel like you're the greatest of them all. But my hidden agenda is to make you believe in my magic mirror on the wall. I celebrate and wear Kings Clothing while watching him fall. Then I'll take his Throne, and I stand tall. I'll take over his crown and steal his Queen. Tricking her Mind and make her feel like I'm the true supreme. I make her forget that she's a jewel more precious than Royalty. I'll make her mine, and demand her loyalty. I'll tell you that I'm religious, I'm a god who saves you from your hell. But the reality is, I worship me and the d-e-v-i-l. I'll forever be in your memory, as a part of your testimony. My name is Jester the Mind Molester, and this is My Story.

WARNING TO KINGS AND QUEENS! They play with your mind and your soul. Learn who you're dealing with, utilize the word no. They play the part of a King very well. Pay close attention to the stories they tell. But you'll know a Real King, by the way he Leads and Teaches. He elevates and empowers, his people while destroying jesters, pheasants, who leaches. (Know The Difference) So take inventory of yourself, and tell God thank you. Because You're Loved, Blessed and Valued.

Dwayne J. Torres

God, You Mean More To Me

I am not perfect by any means, but it doesn't excuse my attitude or my extremes. If they followed me and I lead them astray. Please accept my sincere apologies, I cannot live in yesterday. I want to move forward so we can have a better future. I also need for you to understand, that I was deceived by a soul consumer. Trapping my spirits into his demonic games. Making me believe that he knows my name. Again, I'm not making excuses for what I've caused, I'd still like to have my Father, hope all is not lost. Hear my sincerity as it sings through me. It's letting you know that you mean more to me.

You've opened my eyes; Your Spirit woke me. So I prayed to you and spoke clearly. I prayed hoping that love, will display of who I am. Thank you Father, for allowing me to be, a Kingdom Man. Yes, I wished that I could do so much more. But Father, you always have something greater in store. You told me to trust as you order my steps. Told me to remember all of the promises that you've kept. I didn't believe that I was worthy but YOU, said Yes. You said that you can still use me, and be blessed. Thank You Father for My Royalty Being. I Love You God, and You Mean More to Me. Today I renounce My Sinful Nature, I'm giving up that throne. I want you to show the World that you are God, and God Alone. I may be an Earthly King, but I'm not Sovereignty. I'm just a vessel who loves God, who lives in Victory and not demonic poverty. Hey, don't get me wrong, (Brothers and Sisters) you are a part of this. Just forsake your pride and have your sins dismissed. Jesus already did it for you at the Cross. Live Free, He Already Paid the Cost.

He paid it with his own Blood. That's why a standard is raised against the enemy's flood. You are Royalty and so am I, we are all the Apple of God's Eye. Trust and believe your purpose will be achieved. Release your burdens and your stress. Look into your mirror, you'll see Blessed.

Dwayne J. Torres

He Who Finds A Wife

Is she a Queen? Yes. What does that mean? I'm Blessed. Are You Her King? Most Definite. And your job? To Love, Serve, and Protect. Why do you Love Her? Because God allowed. God allowed How? Because I told him I'll Take care of her when I made That Vow. So where's her crown? It's in her soul. Why there? Because My Love will keep it's Hold. Cool, so what now? I'll continue to Bring. Bring what? My Gift from God for her heart to sing. Thanks for the information, but I don't understand. How can this Queen Love this common man? Because I'm a part of God's Plan. Being her King by following his command. By displaying Love when you put away pride. And how Great Love can be through God's Eye. No man can asunder what God put together. If you ask if I Love Her, I'll say Forever.

I Carry You

While you were sleeping, I've prayed. Praying that your blessings aren't delayed. But that's not the only thing I do. Every day and Night My Soul and I Carry You. I take in your pain, by being your umbrella to your rain. Oh, I'm sorry let me explain, I don't do this for a sexual gain. I do it out of Love and Responsibility. Because God allowed me to have the Opportunity. To Love a Queen, Beautiful, Classy and Pure. Which is why I take in all that you endure. No not by any means I'm not here to replace God. I will stand in front of a firing Squad. Just so that you are protected, never leave your heart or spirit neglected. We have a soul connection, you know that Royalty affection. It's not easily broken; my action and words have spoken. It displays all that I do, I show you love when I carry you.

I didn't always get it right, which is why I learned how to fight. Against Wolves in Sheep's Clothing, by using God's Anointing. I won't allow your World to Crumble, I'll keep your Enemies Humbled. By always being 5 steps ahead, leaving them speechless and shaking their heads. Spiritual Foods you're always fed, putting your mistakes behind you, it's dead. Renovating My Palace, being free from drama and Malice. You wear My Crown it's a Perfect Fit. I'm Your Forever Covering, Spiritually and Physically Equipped. Being a King is not the only thing that I do. Serving and Protecting My Queen, which is why I Carry You. Two Candles Lighting as One, celebrating victories we've won. Fighting Enemies who don't fight fair. Takes me to the limit and don't even care. But they don't understand my strength, with No Armor in sight. Kryptonite can't even stop My Superman Faith and Might. I Love Being a part of a true Majesty. Blessed by God our Father, and Sovereignty. There is a lot to the table that I bring. Serving My Queen with Love from this Debonair King. You stimulate me with your beauty and intellect, leaving me with moments of joy that I'll never forget. As you can see, Loving is not all that I do. I Pray, Fight, and Soar, while I Carry You.

My Her

She's My sunrise in my darkness. Make me hustle the hardest. She's an incredible artist. I'll truly go the farthest. I'll go through the storms and rain, I take in her pain. Just so she'll see that my love is sustained. I call her My Queen, a reality to my dream. A Goddess Motivation walking. Loving This King Debonair Talking. Not a shame to Showcase, her love in my heart it's placed. A Destiny Traveling, our Love Unraveling. Sure, we've both made mistakes, owning up is all it takes. To Forgive May be hard, but you just leave it up to God. Never giving more than you can bare. His Love shows that he cares. My Dedication to her is for her appeal. Letting Her Know My Love is Real. While I Love her completely, She Loves Me Virtuously. I'll keep fighting until I reach all successes. I Love You So, My Queen.

Dwayne J. Torres

My Queen, Her King

I did not come to tear you apart. I came to Love you and protect your heart. I did not come to judge you or your past. I want to lead you into your Destiny, with the hope our Love will last. I want to share my kingdom to demonstrate what I have to offer. Being what God wants me to be, while I'll meet you at the altar. A place where I go to God and make a vow. To complete my mission to make you Queen, and give you my crown. I'll support you, showcase you, not to brag nor for conceit. I just want to tell the world how I appreciate you and how my life is complete. Please let me pick you up, and wrap you around my wings. Lift up your esteem, with Love and security I'll bring. I cannot promise perfect, but I promise care. As long as your love don't change, I will always be there. You are the bright star in which I'm willing to commit. To Serve, to cherish, to provide, while we submit. Not a form of dominance, but a form of allegiance. A partnership, Togetherness while with God we're living obedience. Forever I'll be your King, serve with complete Solidarity. Foretelling a dream, a vision with clarity. You're the Woman who holds the key to my Heart. I'm admiring your intelligence and your smarts. A Demonstration of An Inspiration. An Appreciation, and My Motivation. A sight of pleasure, her soul and spirit I'll treasure. I'll be her protection, write poems as My Dedication. I'm her King who will declare and decree. I Love Her, My Queen Reality.

Before We Met

They say men don't get lonely, because we have so many women to choose. Hit as many as you can, you have nothing to lose. Men look weak when they express of care and love. Being called soft and sensitive even to the point of, questioning himself is he truly a man? Do I have be this Non-Descript for a woman's attention? I don't understand. I was always taught that a woman is a man's pride and joy. To give her love so she can distinguish between a Man and a boy. So I started to get motivated of becoming a Master of Being a King. To discover more of myself and what Royalty I will Bring. I've studied my heart to let go of damaged goods. Took total inventory and prayed to God Like I Should. This is why when you first laid eyes on me, you felt we've met before. Because your spirit immediately intertwined with mine, something we wanted to explore. Removing all of the iniquities especially the ones we kept. I never knew the beauty of love, way before we've met.

You told me of your past, and how in mind you still lived there. My goal is to release all of your tensions, by showing you how much I care. You've brought in some baggage, and I brought drama too. But we escaped and then we embraced. Those issues never bloomed. Because of our foundation was founded and Blessed. By God with his Heavenly Angels, that's why the test. Of those whom came before us, and love became a myth. We thought we couldn't get any better than those who we were with. But never say never because you're making God laugh. Because he knows us better, and whom to put in our path. But they were just a chapter in our Biography. Your past maybe a factor, but it doesn't apply to me. It's just all an experience that you kept.

That happened all before we met. Now eyes have not seen, nor ears have heard. Now that I'm your King, Our God will give you all that you deserve. And that's a whisper to your heart and spirit of Love. After God, there's you first, and no one else above. So I share my world with you and love you like the Queen that you are. Don't ever be afraid of where we are going, no matter how far. I will lead to places with God as our navigator. Your mind, I want to explore and be your stimulator. I couldn't Imagine my life without you and how you complete me. To enjoy our life together, and it hasn't been easy. But I know what Love is, and I Thank God for us he's Kept. My life is more whole, than before we met.

Inspirationally Redeemed

She's a Keeper

I never knew a Love Like this, although I Loved Before. It was Nobody but God, he knew of what I had in store. My ultimate goal is to have peace of mind. To be a blessing to those whose joy they want to find. But nothing like having a woman, who walks your every step. Don't criticize you of your promises you haven't kept. She's the Warden who holds you down. Never keeping you bound. Stimulates while talking, a Goddess Walking. More than a Beauty Queen, who's not all about the Green. Your Better Half, who calms your wrath. A treat to the eyes, Loves you Why? You're her King, more loving she'll bring. More than a Gift, and there to uplift. Return Love only required, while she inspires. For you to be the best, while not settling for less. She'll bring you joy, may even give you a boy. To carry on your name, Loving You with no shame. Even if you're not her fantasy, she'll say oh how fine is he. Writes your name on blank cards, your heart she'll guard. By praying for your protection, giving much attention and affection. If you don't have one like her, then she's a dreamer. If you have one like her, than she's a keeper.

She could be your hustler, or your Bonnie to your Clyde. She'll turn you back to Dr. Jekyll when you're Mr. Hyde. You would want to be the salt to her ocean, a Beauty Poetry in Motion. She'll move mountains, Love flowing like fountains. A Mother's care, beautiful whether short, long, or no hair. She's a friend till the end, your heart she wants to mend. A Wonder Woman to your Superman. Your support group to say you can, declares you as her man. A Love Supreme, never too much or extreme. She always laughs at your jokes no matter how corny. Wants to help you on your journey. Makes your day sweeter, Loving You deeper, and never a sleeper. She's The Woman of your life, you should make your wife. She's a Keeper.

Who Am I?

I'm A Soul Survivor

Nasty, No Vision, Insecure Man, I was called. Procrastinator, Terminator, Fat boy, the Devil Loves it when I crawl. I Stopped trying to be good, what's the use? Because My reward is far greater than any demon's abuse. Couldn't feed my family, but Wife and Kids still smiled. Because they knew that trouble was only there for a little while. Mistakes were made, and were times I've failed. But Jesus died for my sins, so my soul always made bail. I've won and lost some battles, but Never Lost a war. Because My Faith is uneasily broken, My Purpose never goes ignored. I cannot stay down, it's not a part of My DNA. God gave me his word, that there will be brighter Days. (Haggai 2:9) I bit off more than I can chew, but I swallowed My Pride. No Weapon was formed against me, Because God is on my side. (Isaiah 54:17) What He started up in me, will conclude and finish. So all of that fear of uncertainty, must be destroyed and diminished. (Philippians 1:6) My Debt was paid in full, by Jesus' Blood and Power. He released me from my oppressed prison, by saving me from the devourer. My Soul prepared my fight, but it's God who's My Fighter. No principalities can't Ever stop My Praise, because I'm a Soul Survivor.

Am I Still Relevant?

Me: Father God, Sometimes I feel as if my Living isn't a Life, I'm just existing. I care too much about society that My purpose goes missing. Then I mistake others progresses as My failures. Not really understanding their fight are for their treasures. I compare My career to others, thinking that I'm losing. Living depressed and discouraged, which the devil finds amusing. Sometimes I blame you, forgetting that you are God. You can take on any task, and destroying any odds. But I Question, Am I living just to survive? Or am I'm being punished for the sins that I've tried to hide? Never mind the favors on me that's daily bestowed. I've truly forgotten about the promises that you've told. I'm living in a world of the materialistic and superficial. If I don't keep up with the Joneses, my world becomes so critical. Am I being a procrastinator, or just Hesitant? Help me Lord to figure it out, am I still Relevant?

God: Why do you Question with such animosity? Why you would feel irrelevant, is Truly Beyond Me. I've created you, Mr. Fearfully, Wonderfully Made. Every Test you're Given, you've passed and made the Grade. Stop believing that you are last in this race. Because when you're at my dinner table, you'll get the first taste. (Psalm 23:5) You don't need to keep with the Joneses because their treasures are temporary. By the time I get through with you, you'll have much more, and a testimony. You're not a procrastinator, but some of your choices had you stymied. Trust me that you'll get it all, within My Timing.

When it comes to Blessing you, I'm never hesitant. Look into your mirror, you'll see purpose, and You're Relevant.

Inspirationally Redeemed

Tired King, Messenger, Developer

Tired King, but Empire Building. Planning and Engaging, Legacy Brewing. I don't know about Your fight, but I know about Mine. Just when he (the devil) thought I'll give up, that's when I'll rise. The King fought a good fight, that's what they'll say. He fought for what he believed in, come what may. If he said that he loves you he meant it from the heart, even when Love is not returned, he never fell apart. But that's the story and life of a King. Fights, Support, Serves, Royalty is his being. Writes down his visions, plans of his dreams. (Habakkuk 2:2) Praise and Serves God along with his Queen. Gives her a life of Royalty, with a Spiritual Affection. Respects her Mind, Body, and Soul, a true Love Connection. My Destiny does not depend on what man say. Just as Long I Do it God's Way. I'm not here for show and tell. I'm here to give a message to prevent you from hell. Today is the Day That the Lord Has Made. Rejoice, Be Glad, The Debt is already paid.

Inspired by Galatians 3:13-15

The Identity Crisis

When you don't remember who you are, in another state of being. Transferring one's mind, Losing Life's meaning. You dismiss your purpose or your process of walking. Forsaking your birth right ain't nothing but the devil talking. You were Born with a cause, but got attracted to sin. Forgetting you've been forgiven, and battles to win. Someway somehow, we've got it all wrong. Believe in yourself, your vitality is strong. You made some mistakes and that's ok. Jesus already forgave you, now be on your way. The devil tries his best to make you suffer, in a mind paralysis. But you must exercise your spirit, start with the Book of Genesis. Equipping oneself with a sword and shield. There's no affliction that God can't heal. You are a child of God, who was placed in the Stars. Trust Me, He Knows who you are. You allow your sins to give you a title. But your true identity is in the Bible. You are God's Child, Fearfully and Wonderfully Made. You May have failed, but always made the grade. When you failed you were growing. Too focused on your trials without knowing. That you have the ability to excel to unlimited greatness. You have authority over snakes, scorpions and fakeness. Take off your mask, because you have a task. To start a Legacy Generation, being a Blessing to All Nations. No longer be a figure with many faces. Get your confidence back on a natural basis. God sent Jesus who has made many sacrifices. So you can stop your suffering, from an Identity Crisis.

Know Who You Are

I talk about seeing your purpose, by looking into your mirror. I also speak of going to God, and getting delivered. I try to get you to understand, that you are a part of God's Plan. Tell him yours, and he will laugh. Work on your Faith and your craft. No, you were not born with a silver spoon in your mouth. You were Born into a Royal Priesthood, so don't you dare fear or doubt. Excellence and Greatness is in your DNA. But we allow our sins to make us believe that our distinction is decayed. When truth of the matter is, Jesus washed it away. We are Naturally Kings/Queens we are not slaves. However, our mind does get enslaved by fleshy thoughts, because we forgot of what we're taught. That we are more than a conqueror standing tall. Delivering and overcoming the devil's pit falls. He invites you to his parties, where glamour appears. But It's a celebration of Carnal Reprobate minded years. It's a set up for a Soul confiscation. Destroying your Empowered Spirits so don't accept his invitation. Look at yourself, have faith and Believe. You already passed the test, so get ready to succeed. It's not as hard as it seems. You're the Reality to God's Favored Dreams. Remove those blinders so you can see. That God made you a King/Queen totally Free. Look My Brothers/Sisters you've come this far. It's truly time to know who you are. You have a purpose among the living. You're God's Earthly Thanksgiving. Know That You were created By Love, Pure and Honest. And that you are not only the blessing, but the promise. You're wonderfully made, just like the Sun and the Stars. You're Royalty, Beautiful, Loved, and Blessed, Know Who You Are.

Validation

You've already been Validated by the Blood of The Lamb. You were Born and Forgiven. Now it's time for me to tell you a lil about Your livin'. Your Validation was upon your Creation. You're a demonstration of Love, a walking Education. Your purpose is to leave a Legacy Generation. Look at you, you're God's Celebration. So no need to look for any approval of man's chatter. Because when you were conceived, God already said that you matter. So Remember You're here for a reason, notice you survived every dry season. Famine may have played a role. But you were equipped because God is in Control. So if you can get through a tough situation. God has shown you his manifestation. Which means don't look for man's approval, he has limitations. Look to the one who'll Bless You in front of all Nations. You're a King/Queen, a Blessed Harvest, Your Royalty Reign and obtained. You've been Validated, and Approved by God your Legacy Sustained. VALIDATION!

Look at Me I'm Soaring

I'm taking flight over the mountains and the seas. I'm not going to slow down because of disfunction or disease. A disease that is curable, just need to have faith that's more durable. The disease is called fear, causing me to fly low and having my dreams disappear. But I was not designed for any hesitations, my wings spread wide to reach all destinations. I cannot control the air, and I ain't supposed to live in a nightmare. Winds blows in my face, trying to hold me back and stay safe. Although it may be comfortable, but if I stay, I'll get vulnerable. Open to an advice from a pigeon or a Crow, they're smart, but their diction is slow. It'll just ruin my flow and I cannot grow.

I am not equipped to be at ease. I'm expecting to rise above and succeed. I have a vision that exceeds man. Which means that I see trouble beforehand. I don't fly above it, I just go through. Because God placed it there so my faith can renew. To totally trust in him, releasing all anxiety and win. My will to win is more dangerous than a Lion's Roar. Which is why God equipped My Wings to fly and Soar. I'm the one you look up to and sets the tone. Reaching all Achievements and Milestones. You'll know about me and My Story. Because I'll be the one Praising and Giving God the Glory! With my Capabilities, my Conviction and Confidence restoring. Take a good Look at Me, I'm Flying and Soaring.

My Name is...

I can make you climb Mountains, swim across the seas. I'm a Baby's Smile, I'm a master's degree. I can speak many languages, I come prepared. I'm your Hype Man, saying no other can compare. I'm so right for you, God likes what I do. No, I'm not temptation, My Name is Inspiration.

I give you a vision, I give you a hope. I'm the one who don't accept failure nor the word nope. There's no other option other than more shopping. For will and designation with much anticipation. I'm the vision with a decision. My Name is Motivation.

Today is My Birthday, just like Yesterday and Tomorrow. Reason why I die and rebirth every day, is because of sorrows. I'm created from a greater source, and you'll never understand why. I'm the truth, and I cannot lie. Your belief is My strength and weakness. If I'm used correctly, you'll love my uniqueness. I'm your story from a higher authority and a living testimony. I've cured many Diseases, I'm the one who God Pleases. I'm your greatest gift and your biggest fan, so let me tell you who I am. My Name is Faith.

My Name is....2

I know you, I Live inside. I'm Faith and Fear Combined. I'm your confidence and confusion. I'm Temptation wrapped up as an illusion. You'll never understand, and you don't know why. I'm your truth, as well as your lie. I'm the one who engulfs your mess. Then once I'm finished, you'll be Blessed. I'm your trial and tribulation. I'm your benefit to your determination.

Then I'll make you appear weak when you're bold. Like poker, I'm a Royal Flush, and will make you fold. I dare you to try me, heck I want you to win. You get promoted, and get to live again. Hey, my friend, don't even get upset or stressed. You'll make it by the way, My Name is Test.

Consider it pure joy, my brothers and sisters, whenever you face trials of many kinds, because you know that the testing of your faith produces perseverance. Let perseverance finish its work so that you may be mature and complete, not lacking anything - James 1:2-4

My Name is....3

Hello Beautiful/Handsome how are you doing? It's been a while so a new thrill is brewing. Oh I know all about your story. Let's be real, It has been a lil boring. Allow Me if you will to administer, as I get closer don't mind my slither. I can make your story so great and exciting. By giving you a vision that's so enriching and enticing. You'll feel immortal no matter what laws you break. Feeling that passion and power of freedom, it's yours to take.

Oh come on now, you're my slave pretty much. You'll fall into an ecstasy by just one touch. I know all of your moves, you are so predictable. You can never leave me alone, I'm too irresistible. I can lead the most faithful on a wrong path. So addicting that you'll need rehab. I had to hunt you, at first you weren't an easy prey. I took notice of your desires, then seduced you my way.

I got you in my hands and that's where you'll stay. Until you utilize your Faith, you'll continue to decay. I was Born in the same tree by Adam and Eve. I was so successful by blinding them with my cousin deceive. I don't need to be inspired, because I am what you want in any situation. You called on me, My Name is Temptation. Avoid Me at all Costs.

Inspirationally Redeemed

When I Look at You, I see purpose

An Alluring Sunrise, a Mighty Champion has Surfaced. You can't hide from me, nor you can't lie. I see a testimony, I see your cries. You take pain on a whole new level, you escape it with jokes, you're kind of special. I see your talents, you speak with intelligence. I know your secrets, your fears of ignorance. You give yourself credit, then you find fault. You take your time when you have second thoughts. You are the master to your slave, the tombstone to your grave. You set goals and plan strategically. I see why you've never stopped praying faithfully. I see your lies, I see your truth. I've seen you do things that are beneath you.

You got it going on, despite what you say. You have no idea of the swag you display. I see you rehearse for a job interview, I believe in you. Let Go of all your doubts, fears, and mildew. I've seen this before, you'll get through. I enjoy watching you sing your favorite tune. I didn't come to judge nor hate. God made me for you to reflect and demonstrate. I Must say you're Beautiful/Handsome you Reek Awesomeness and Extremely Superior. I'd like to introduce Myself, I am your Mirror. Now take your picture.

What Next, Where Did I Go Wrong?

Me: Why God?
God: It had a purpose.
Me: And what was That?
God: It's for service.
Me: You mean Church?
God: No, No.
Me: Then What?
God: You'll Know.
Me: Ok, why now?
God: Because you wouldn't move.
Me: Move, where?
God: You wouldn't have approved
Me: Enlighten me, I'm Lost
God: And That's the Cost.
Me: Hey I'm just asking again
Jesus: Remember me, My Friend?
Me: Yes I Remember, but I still don't understand.
God: Don't you know the cost of a man?
Me: Obviously I don't if I keep Questioning? But you give me parables, without even mentioning. I'm stuck and lost, and you say it's a cost. I don't mean to come off all complexed. But where did I go wrong, what next?
Jesus: May I Father, take this one?
God: Sure, My Beloved Son.
Jesus: You've read the book and heard the story. But still

don't see me in every category? I died so you can live. Ok you understand that, so what gives? You are a danger to the devil's camp. Which is why the attacks, and you are amped. If you were not a danger, you wouldn't be so strong. Dare to ask, where did I go wrong? How long will it be, with all of this pain?

Well My Friend, look at all that you'll gain. A weapon of your tongue, so you speak of elevation. A weapon of faith is also motivation. A weapon of trust and Succeeding. Look at what you'll be achieving. A weapon of strength, which is why it hurts. Building up Legacies, and rediscovering your worth. You're way too focused on the mess. Not realizing it's just all progress. Remember all things will work Together. God, Myself, and the Holy Spirit will reign Forever.

You are your Greatest Enemy

How dare I speak such travesty? Speaking of us with such blasphemy. I say us, as if I know you personally. We never spoke before, don't know your personality. But please don't get upset because I speak the truth. We've been fighting our inner demons since our youth. Ok I understand that you love yourself, and you set goals. Not perfect by any means, truth be told. Your greatest fear is totally believing, you are more powerful than what you've been achieving. An inch of self-doubt is the enemy of self-esteem. All it takes is a mustard seed, to live out your dream. You can tell me that you are more than confident, which is great, hallelu. But God allows roadblocks to retract our path, to say it's about him not you. So since we know of ourselves and God knows more, we can achieve anything through him, beyond the door.

Your worst critic is not your neighbor, it is you. Never doubting your gifts, but comparing is something we shouldn't do. Yet we compare our greatest accomplishments with our past. Sometimes it's our situation hoping we could outlast.

Saying "I don't live there no more, and looking at what God will have in-store. I'm no longer in a state of me, because I truly believe totally. I am free from doubt and fear; those things are gone, it disappeared. I can't believe how I ever lived there, I wasn't going anywhere. So when I look at what I've achieved, I realized that I can do it, just needed a reprieve. Knowing what I know was half the battle, while destroying snakes that rattle. If I don't fear them when I already have Frenemies, I will continue to be My Greatest Enemy.

Understand it's not for subtraction, but to appreciate every satisfaction. Remembering it's for my calling, not my falling. God did this for me, to totally depend on him, for my Destiny."

Dwayne J. Torres

A Kingdom Man

I am a Warrior, I fight my battles on my knees. I am a Conqueror, I overcame every Adversity. I am a King, I am Royalty. I am a Praying Man, under God's Authority. In other words, I am a Kingdom Man. A Fighter, A Conqueror, an Overcomer, and not your Candy Man. My Faith becomes Life, my scars shows my strife. I live this life to live again, forever praying for my family, enemies, and friends. I'll say it again, in case you didn't comprehend. I'm always standing after storms and winds. I broke out from the Devil's Hand. God then declared me as a Kingdom Man. You tried to stop my calling, you tried to do all that you can. You cannot stop my mission and purpose, because I am a Kingdom Man. Allow me to reintroduce myself, as you stand confused and unclear. I am a powerful force under the influence of God, the one you greatly fear. This power that was given to me, was given since my Day of birth. I didn't realize its power, because you told me that it has no value or worth. But I'm glad to know that you are nothing but a deceiver. God Blessed me with this power, and I am Forever a Believer. Once I've discovered it's true meaning, the life of being a Kingdom Man. You tried to deliver every opposition, and hoped that I'll never Understand. That I am a King and My Kingdom is formed on a Blessed Land. Although there were Giants, I still progressed and got Blessed, then became the Man. The one who you feared, and tried to take out. I am a Praying God-Fearing Warrior Man, something you don't know about. So don't try to stop something that you can't kill. For I am a Kingdom Man, Blessed and Made under God's will.

Believer

Do You Believe What You Perceived?

Have you looked into your mirror, and found the answers you seek? Have you drawn any conclusions, or was your vision very Bleak? Did you somehow leave with confidence, or was your mind in a prison? Did you hesitate on your craft, or seek others for your decision? Was it a trick of the mind, of failures of your past? Are you ready for a future, or believe in its task? How do you plan the goals you want to achieve? Or Do You Truly Believe, in What You Perceived?

No one has a gift like you, so why fear or doubt? Is it too much trouble, for you to figure it out? How can you discover of the worlds ahead? Truth of the matter, your dreams are not dead. Don't use your age as an excuse, to prevent your pursuit. It began in your mind, like your seeds it will uproot. No matter how many books, or degrees you received. It'll be no good, if you don't believe what you perceived.

Whether you operate on Faith or believe in Fate. The Future ahead, is yours to take. I for one am what they call a man with a plan. A vision to the quest, all within God's Hands. He gave me the Green Light to do my impossible. He also gave me the strength, to withstand all of the obstacles. I want you to believe in you like I believe in me. We could pray and stand together and set our minds free. From the prison of things that kept us bound, to hold back ourselves, and never reach higher ground. You can and will be more than what you believe. You just have to trust in all that you will perceive.

The Esteem of Others

Hey, pleased to meet you, I am glad that we could connect. I'm sorry to sound corny, but I strongly believe we've already Met. You look Beautiful/Handsome and have it going on. Not to sound corny again, but you're a fairytale Once Upon. I'm so glad you love my compliment, that was my intent. To get to know you better, you must have been sent. Oh me? I'm just a squirrel trying to get a nut. Not really into this thing called life, it's a lot of smut. I look at people, see the bags they carry. They walk like it's all good, but you can tell they're not happy. It's obvious that they have a purpose. All awhile they play with their hearts like a three-ring circus. If they only knew that there's Royalty planted inside. Being the King/Queen that they are, allowing God to be their guide. They shouldn't compare each other's talents and physique. They are wonderfully made, God's Greatest Masterpiece. I could encourage them with my walk and the words I say. But they will never comprehend with what I'm saying, if sadness is displayed. Somethings just can't be hidden, even if we're not admitting. That the day to day puts our mind in a haze. We've compared to a fantasy, while figuring Destiny. Keeping up with the Joneses, hoping no one notices. The pain we try to hide, not allowing pettiness to slide. People, can't you see that I'm your Brother? Let's stop living through the Esteem of Others. Be the Glorious Elevation raising up Legacy Generations.

A Promise to live Forever, loving yourself is more clever. Being the Father or Mother teaching a nation, not live through The Esteem of Others. Love Always, Your Brother

Blessed

To be Blessed means to be tried. It also means something has to go, especially pride. You'll delay your Blessings by holding a grudge. To someone or something, but who am I to Judge? Sometimes we believe that Blessings comes in form of our desires. Please remove from that way of thinking, you're just playing with fire. This Favor God gives us is not just for us to hold. You're supposed to pay it forward, so another testimony can be told. You are a blessing to God and to The World. Because you are His precious jewel, valued more than Diamonds or Pearls. Let's go back when I talked about Fire. His ways are better, and his thinking is much higher. When we hear No, sometimes we want an explanation. We must trust that his path, is to a greater destination. We can plan around our goals, but with a Blessing wouldn't be plausible. However, with God's guidance, we can achieve the Impossible. Each waking day is a daily walk of experiences and lessons. Sometimes We may have to go out of our way to be a blessing. A smile or a simple good morning could make someone's day. We don't know their situation, so a mere hello goes a long way. You're going out or coming in, a remission from sin. Remember who you are, you're one of God's rising stars. A King or A Queen, you're his high esteem. A Diamond in a rough, worth more than enough. An Apple to his eye, Loves You by and by. You're a Living Testimony Extraordinary. Nothing Less, Rose above mess. You've passed every test, so you are Blessed.

Dwayne J. Torres

Prayer

Many don't understand its concept, nor its purpose. It's open communication, it does its service. It can reach places beyond, it can open locked doors. It can reach the ears of God, the one who never ignores. Some say it's a facade, some say it doesn't work. Many don't know how to, so they sound like a jerk. But they should never under estimate its power, for its very groundbreaking. To build up your relationship with God, it's even breathtaking. How Can You not speak to God, when he doesn't Lie? He answers all your questions, especially the ones that begins with why. You go to him, come as you are. He will not condemn you, you're his rising star. He knows you better than you know yourself, even the number of your hair. He whispers to your soul, while the devil screams God is not there. But you can ignore his screams by kneeling down. Expressing your pain and afflictions, while Jesus intercedes for your crown.

Oh yes there's always a cross you have to bare. But God will resurrect your dialect, all through prayer. When you go to God, it's music to his ears. Your pride and sins are forgiven, while releasing all fears. Please don't be mistaken, you are not forsaken. You may believe that you don't deserve, because you don't go to church and serve. But you can go to God in prayer, showing you how much he cares. Many charlatans lie, so why Bother. Wolves in sheep's clothing, but there is GOD, He's your Father. There is no sin that he can't cover. He'll surround you with other praying sisters and brothers. You are stronger and greater than you believe. Prayer gets answered, ain't nothing that you can't achieve.

Within his will, he knows the deal. A communication to a great inspiration. A Warrior's Weapon, the devil is threatened. A talk with God, a Beautiful Promenade. Prayer is stronger than any man's might. Prayer is comfort before good night. An awakening Morning Ceremony. My Forever Testimony. There's peace beyond this message, which I had to share. Reaching God's Heart, when you go to God in Prayer.

Dwayne J. Torres

The True Warrior

I appear to be weak when cry, I look like a Clark Kent on the outside. But you have no idea to what kind of Man I am, even the devil tries to hide. Tries to blind me with depression and insecurities, but even that can't stop. The fight in me won't quit unless I'm the one on top. I'm made of steel, no I ain't Superman. I am The True Warrior, even when I fall, I still Stand. Please don't get me confused with a man in a cape. He is great in his own right, but it's kryptonite he can't escape. You see I was created by life experiences, with layers of perils and strive. Many tried to kill me, but I still survived. Every mountain was high, and every valley was low. Won every battle because Jesus covered me with his Blood and saved my soul. Outside you'll see me and call me a Kingdom Man. Truth be told, I'm The True Warrior strictly under God's Command. I'm not the only True Warrior that's walking on this Earth. There are other Brothers Like me, just need to recognize their worth. I was made to build as well as love and protect. Building up Kingdoms with the Soldier Affect. Never take for granted of the strength inside me, for even the Greatest Fall. So I must stay humble while continuing to stand tall. My sword is prayer, My Faith is Shield. Victory won Battle Scars healed. Always notorious until victorious. Forever fighting never dying. Breaking down all barriers, helping worriers. It's me (Your Name) The True Warrior.

The Virtuous Woman

The Virtuous Woman is a woman of value, a Queen in her own right. A Blessed Woman of God, with a bright shined Light. She is admired by men, but her place is with a Kingdom Man. Who Leads with a blessed heart, and welcomes her to his Promise Land. She Loves not to make him weak, but to make him strong. She stands in the gap of prayer, because she knows where she belongs. She never has to doubt, nor she has to fear. She has such a trust in God, knowing that he's always near. With self-respect she walks with her head up high. Never has to bow in defeat because she knows why. Victory is automatic no matter what happens. Either A lesson is learned, or it's a wrap, we win. She's The First Mother, Teacher, Preacher, this World has ever Known. A Blessing to us all, while holding down her own. Virtuous Woman, a beautiful sight to see. Always bringing out the winner in you and me. A Kingdom Man's Appreciation. A devil's Frustration. Father God, I thank you for all your Blessings, delivering us from hell and man. For seeing fit to Bless us all, with a Virtuous Woman.

Dwayne J. Torres

The Journey

I have too long of a journey, to go back now. What's before me is much better than what's behind me. A Destiny too Great, that if I don't stay focused, I will miss my promise. Inspiration will start the ignition, Preparation will shift the gears, Determination, will give its Drive. Faith will be my gas, and Appreciation will be my pitstops, Fortitude will keep me Going. Thankfulness, God Fearing, Talent trading, Grateful to God Goodness and Mercies is my Destination. For Greatness, Abundance, Humbleness and Integrity will be my Dwelling.

Whose Life Is It Anyway?

Me: Who am I to You? Am I the favored or the disappointed? Am I the backslider, or the Anointed? Am I the Simple or the meek? Am I the wonderfully made or the incomplete? Am I the blessed or the shamed? Does The Book of Life have My Name? Am I the Deacon or The Preacher? Am I the Layman or The Teacher? Who am I, to whom I Pray? If not me, Whose Life Is It Anyway?

God: My Precious Jewel of a Child, why would you question thee? We spend Quality time, and you still don't see? When I made you, I broke the mold. Wrote the Greatest book that was ever sold. You'll have a testimony that needs to be told. I'll give you a message, and it never gets old. But why would you question an answer you already know? I give you a sign every day, no need for a show. I gave you a gift so that you can share. To be a blessing to those all whom I care. The Blessing was set, before you arrived. Look at all of the mess, you've survived. Don't you think that you've been had? They are forgiven so don't stay sad. I Love it, in this convo you said me. But I want everyone who reads to see. What I'm saying to you, I say to all. I will surely catch you, when you fall. If there are answers to which you seek. It's in My word so take a peek. You are Loved and a part of Royalty. I will protect you with Love and Dignity. I gave this Life, to be a Blessing in this World.

To share your gifts while defeating, the snares of the underworld. You are more than a Conqueror with a Warrior Heart. It's always been your Life, from the start. Now go in peace, and live out your Blessings and live free. Continue to tell the world, of messages from me. You are the appointed and anointed.

The Preacher and The Teacher. And acknowledge your life without shame. Do it out for Love, and not for Fame. You are My Precious Soldier, strong and complete. My Warrior victorious always, never in defeat. Whose Life? It's Yours. I Love You.

The Power of Unity

I came with baggage of mess. You came with baggage of pain. Together We can take this test. So our peace can be sustained. We can go on many levels. We can fly very high. We can defeat many devils, weakness won't apply. I give you my strength and might. You always have my back. Together we will win the fight. From all of the devil's attacks. I am your Rock, you are My Diamond. Stronger than Fort Knox. Rising above Highlands. You hold me up, while holding it down. Beautiful without make up, skin of Dark Brown. I am your King, strengthened by prayer. Power is what I bring, while showing that I care. We don't need words to uncover, just a new world to discover. A form of togetherness, while destroying the devil's mess. No need to stress, because God Loves us Best. Standing on the Promise not wishes, I'm Your Man You're My Misses. Putting away inferior, while standing Superior. A Queen in your right, A King with all might. Together we will fight, let's take this opportunity. Us against the World, for there is Power in Unity.

ABOUT THE AUTHOR

As an ordained minister, Dwayne J. Torres has a ministry of love and support throughout the community. He has a practical approach that allows his message to reach people from all backgrounds. His unique way of speaking to the people, has understanding, making individuals feel comfortable to come as they are, with no judgement, and no restrictions. He uses his gifts to help those that are searching for spiritual guidance, and takes special interest in all those that he opens his door to.

Dwayne has over 20 years of marketing and public relations experience. His knowledge of personal mentorship and motivational speaking has been an asset in helping families and individuals. As an Insurance broker and ordained minister, Dwayne has taken his passion for helping people to promote the services of personal Insurance through various media outlets, and community centers. His expertise as a Licensed Broker and a motivational speaker, go hand in hand with the excellent service he provides to the people he helps every day. He combines his ministry with his knowledge of insurance to bring to the community a new voice that will make a difference today.

With his first published book of inspirational poetry, Dwayne J. Torres aspires to touch the souls and hearts of the broken and confused. And give a message of love that will leave the presence of God with all who encounters it. His motivational words of truth and wisdom will not only inspire, it will change and uplift the lives who thirst for the knowledge that comes from within the spirit.